A POPULAR PLAY
NEW AND SELECTED POEMS

CLEATUS RATTAN

Texas Review Press
Huntsville, Texas

FIRST EDITION

Requests for permission to acknowledge material from this work should be sent to:

Permissions
Texas Review Press
English Department
Sam Houston State University
Huntsville, TX 77341-2146

Acknowledgements:

Some of these poems appeared in slightly altered forms or under different titles in *Amherst Review, Concho River Review, Cedar Rock, descant, New Mexico Humanities Review, New Texas* ('91, '92, '98, '99, '00, '01), *Pawn Review, Poetry Northwest, Pony Express(ions), Sam Houston Literary Review, Red Rock Review, Red Owl, RE Arts and Letters, Sands, Sanscrit, Sewanee Review, Southwest Review, Sulphur Review, TEX!, Texas Anthology, Texas Review, Vanderbilt Review, Windhover* ('03-'06), *Wormwood Review,* and *Yearbook of American Poetry* (1985) and the following books: *Free of the Flesh* (Red Lion Press), *Funerals for Sparrows* (Trilobite Press), *130 Miles to Dallas* (Texas Review Press), *The Border* (Texas Review Press), *Take Your Time Coming Home* (Texas Review Press).

Cover design courtesy of Nancy Parsons, Graphic Design Group.

Front-cover graphic: photos by Cleatus Rattan, composite by Alphagraphics (Eastland, TX).

Library of Congress Cataloging-in-Publication Data

Rattan, Cleatus, 1935- author.
  [Poems. Selections]
  A popular play : new and selected poems / Cleatus Rattan. -- Edition: first.
      pages cm
  ISBN 978-1-68003-026-6 (pbk. : alk. paper)
  1. Ranch life--Texas, West--Poetry. I. Title.
  PS3618.A88A6 2015
  811'.6--dc23
                                        2015003442

For Connie as always.

CONTENTS

A Popular Play

Will

Family Vacation in the Mountains

The Great Doak Walker

Saddle Up

Anticipation

A POPULAR PLAY

NEW AND SELECTED POEMS

A POPULAR PLAY

MYTH

(How I Became a Student)

Driven from the bliss of high school,
freshmen players consulted
about ascending the depth charts.
Horrified to provoke greater varsity wrath,
some argued against an uprising.
What could be worse? Plutonian frowns,
hanging in pandemonium?

Tears of self-sympathy made me fierce
to fight abandonment to even lower
depths. Falsely vowing no fear
of one darting back, I faked
two blockers into believing
their runner had gone wide,
spun into the hole like a spider
climbing for life, stepped up, raised
my shoulder into the future
all-pro running back's chest.

Confounded, my vision slowly clearing,
I saw the leviathan coach gliding
toward me. I struggled to stand,
noticed the RB stumbling, unsure. I smiled
crookedly until Coach floated by me,
stunned the star back who saw himself
in coach's eyes through his face mask.
"You gonna let this goddamned
little freshman do this to you?"
I dropped my eyes to the coach's feet.
Ah, but that's a myth I thought.
Hope abandoned, all smiles stopped forever.

A Popular Play

Only a few seconds left and I, third rate
actor, was sent in to the stage
where I was not the primary lamb.

Teiresias saw it all so clearly, the message
came to me. Too proud to know, I flicked
my hands up in lights and pulled it snugly

to my chest, certain of destiny. Deftly out
then in and a would be hero fell, groping
for me, no hand upon him. Breathing deeply,

already inflated as the globe, I saw Achilles
come to conflict through the last
Hector. Tantalizing him, sure of Athena,

I came close, picked up speed Hermes envied
and cut at an angle only gods know. But
one tip of one finger of the man down

touched my toe or was it my heel?
I rolled in the green meadow to see my goal
ten leagues away. Forty thousand ampitheaterans

moaned as if of one lung. It was high tragedy.
In all my dreams I see helmeted warriors
waiting, smirking. And in Thebes,

the series of old men who couldn't
find their way to where the three roads
cross, saw that play or say they did.

They smile yet. I must bear it all.
It was clear. It was meant to be. Curses.

C'EST NE PAS

Dream of poems in the mouth and hands
of some sweet tippy-toeing dancer
and images of flowers and white wigs

expand into fields of Wordsworthian
twinkling stars thick as ninth graders,
staring at their shoes, infected

with 100 lines of embarrassment,
sullen smoke pouring from their eyes,
reaching skies resolved to get even with lines

of their ellipse on the head of some esthete,
frail as vows of love embroidered
in handkerchiefs, spotted in the blood

of consumptive Garbow's black and white
dainty little coughs that rack no shoulders,
puff no hair from her thin body, as she

consumes hot bisques, room-temperature
black wine, turning liquid eyes into opaque bourbon
cruets, and she fails to see the point of light

coming, bringing the word like renewal,
reverberating thin waves through lead panes
of the stars in explosions she feels

that have not burned out; no constellation
of a disassembled life requires poems,
only chaotic reorganization under pinpricks

of light from dark dark skies hiding consolation
in my form lying beside her strewn with the smoke-like
dust of other poems of another dusk.

AGAIN FOR THE FIRST TIME

The fire has to be filched and bright spots,
flares showed the way down the path
to the pool—a perfect place for filching.
The way darkens now under the lights

of the shopping center. Walgreen's Pharmacy
with all its enticing signs, blandishments
with pictures, covers, yet fails to hide
the dimly lighted path couples barefooted down,

now covered by foot-scraping, burning,
summer concrete. Those dripping nights,
flushed, bright as motion lights surprising
wanderers, and the water that ran down arms,

legs, spurred growth of prickly
bougainvillea around a circular pool,
and felt so slick and refreshing,
the embarrassed water ran off,

ran away, but returns, not in cycled flowers,
but in moments not buried by Starbucks.
Memories rarely fail to return to old divine places.

ALMOST THE LAST RESORT

The ladies of late afternoon lie in rows
endless as stars in space-filled vacuums.
They drag their fingers in water,
call to servant boys for refreshment.
Not one mentions wind tunnel
looks, creaselessly lifting them out of time.

They are forever beautiful, tucked
away from light—these old geese
who preen, hide their heads under big-brims,
and rarely fly with the young ganders, called
for service, whose pheromones scent the night.

Something strange speeds by them like meteorite dust
visible to the naked eye, perhaps spreading seed
to the occasional body in space.

AVE MARY

When I was a kid, with short hair and a commission
reposing special trust, confidence in me,
I played a serious game one year,
hunting in a land far away,
   missed some things.

My girl was a stewardess, not a flight attendant,
for AA. Panting hard, after eternity in-country,
I arrived at her hotel in San Diego one noon,
slowed my breath, asked for her. All signs
and the clerk pointed to a house phone.
The desk and phone vibrated with
incoming you could breathe
   like napalm.

A "Mr. Maverick" had descended from a golf course,
sweaty in a blue Banlon shirt, a little alligator
on his left breast pocket that would become
a polo player. I had never seen him
or heard about him, but understood
he excited people. A bellboy,
close to the end of his path,
bent beneath B's
burden of clubs,
genuflected
with every
   step.

I mentioned this moment to my un-uniformed girl.
She dressed, took a deeper breath than I knew,
reverently incanted a name
I didn't know, can't forget,
hurried to the desk, sighed
   he was not there.

During the dark of the moon, and in the room
with little sparkling lights
that illuminated no one,
   we saw him.

Mr. Maverick was in the bar with three couples
all sneaking shots at him
in the mirror. He acted
   wounded.

Satiated with wine, my lady almost
crossed herself and missed the
moment. Unsatisfied, she
pulled my sleeve,
let go the cruet,
   to leave.

The obsequious bellboy of the morning processional
matched our attempted tip-toe out.
Bowed, the acolyte censered the
bar with a striking, sleek,
blond, uniformed
AA stewardess,
unknown to my
worshipful
   woman.

"Mr. Maverick," the bellboy said,
"Mary here would like to
meet you." Many years,
many embarrassments
later, those words
remember me,
   hang on.

Mr. Jimmy's cold, cold stare from the mirror
froze the room. He swung slowly around
on his stool, his alligator switching
from right to left, looked Mary up,
down deliberately, completed a
revolution, returned his gaze,
said nothing. I dropped
my head, refused
   to look

for the "boy's" face, heard, still
hear, Mary's Doppler high
heels picking up
    speed.

The room thawed. Sweat poured
from the mirror. We rose in a
silent elevator, staring
    through opaque glass.

BEFORE FRIDAY CONFLICTS

After Cornell correct school songs,
we come to the un-singable doggerel
where we affirm and reaffirm praise
for flares we see in the stadium's early lights
when we feel so brave and free,
and proud, yet further exhorted
to chants and other incantations

before someone instructs the Almighty
ubiquitous how he or she might want to help,
including the rain we need. No fighting,
drinking or driving after drinking, only designated
good fellowship for the rites teaching children
to appreciate appropriate bellicosity,
sanctified by the right ritual

AMEN

BOVINE

Boys, because girls are smarter,
indomitably spend
every collapsing,
retching bit of being
for third place,
for a medal that will grow old alone
in a decaying box,
a medal never to be worn.

The boys strive
as if with gods,
but few are smiled upon
by Hermes.
Athena tends to other matters.

BRING BACK THE CLOWNS

I remember orange peel smiles
when we would stick the rinds in our mouths,
muffling circus music through hidden
teeth normally white as calliope keys.

Goofy grins proclaimed huge orange balloon
mouths, and we laughed as if
we had never sung this way before.

You have gone to some other circus,
and I am no longer capable of true
orange peel tunes. Still, when I am alone,
I'll put an orange peel in my mouth,

stare in the mirror and wonder
why the world is backward
without your music.

Class Work in the Office

The slightly older svelte Kappa
with dark hair and small breasts
sits in front of me, tells me
of an incident in another professor's class.
"You'd never do that," she says
with eyes dark and round
as little chocolate moon pies.
Ten seconds after she shuts my door
I fart, scratch my balls, pick my nose.
Cleansing my fingernail with my hankie,
I congratulate myself on deft handiwork
in a ticklish situation.

CORMORANTS' JOURNEY

Snowbirds come diving down, sliding in
carelessly splatting,
pecking on windows, doors,
building nests, dropping threads,
shards of old nests hanging on their beaks,
claws. Their fluttering white feathers
blocking the sun's puny attempts to break through,
making the streets slick with their droppings
as their baggage slides by,
bumping into place side by side by side.

Odysseus would tramp off to far west Texas,
hankering for firm enchiladas, crusty tacos,
brown eyes, and thin clear skies.

COUCHANT BRYANT, HEADMASTER

In his teak cafetorium, he presided.
In making announcements, about school
functions or bodily ones, his thighs collided,
never knees. Under the thin-topped table,
we watched his flesh flap and flop about
like dolphins playing beside an angled bow.

His eyes were never bigger than his brunch,
and he stuffed all his fold-filled face could crunch
into his famous gut. Three hundred pounds,
excluding chins, would arise. Pink jowls sunk around
a lipless mouth. His booming voice would bellow
imperious commands for silence. Shushing sounds
of flesh rose and slid beneath the ripple's flow

      Boys bulged their eyes, sucked air deep in
with round-lipped awe. Couchant kept syllables trim.

CREATION THEORY

Darling actress, wife,
if I put sweet words
in your mouth,
will you remain
bitter? Will you
trace the swirls
of dialogue
in my ear?

Or will you find
another character,
another part
to play with
in some strange company?

Some new playwright
may create you,
evolve himself
for you, I know
how life comes and goes
serpentining from flicking pens.

DESTINATION

For BS

A man appears at her window,
watching her glancing up occasionally
from magazines pictures of autumn scenes.
Light moth shadows fan
gentle, quick movements of darkness
on her face as she turns and turns
again with the music he can faintly
hear, but he can't dance nimbly
because he cannot remember her
face when he steps back in swirls
of snow to float in music that grows
softer as he dances. He stops,
forgetting the music, the moment.

The woman imagines the man
outside her window, dancing.
She shifts her position, looks out
at the movement as he steps back in snow,
leaving only a brief print.

In her study there is no door;
in snow he turns from her.

In his dreams she follows him
through a green forest.
She does not raise her eyes.

Do I know You?

Now these later years
I can't know you again,
my imago. I'd like to ask
if you remember
how we were then,
but I don't want to know
you don't remember.

How will I know
what I was or never was?
A woman whose fender I dented
last week didn't feel
the bump, she said.

ELEGY FOR A FORMER TEACHER

A screech of tires
in a minor key
and she was gone.

She had been
a music teacher,
a good-looking woman
who taught method
and knew rhythm.

I remember swaying
to her beat
crescendo after crescendo.

Young eighth notes arranged
themselves on the sheet
music just for her.
She played them fast.

A drunken boy in his father's car
the paper said.
Nothing else of note.

EQUALITY: IN AND ON THE COURTS

(The NBA is almost 79% African American)

"Talent, man, talent. Nobody gives you nothin." Comment by a student in response to my question concerning the statistic stated above.

The African American (formerly Black) girl's eyes
snap up quicker than a quark at the word Nigger.
It is the only word she has heard all semester—
though not the only time her frequently sleepy eyes
rolled back. Twain's times, however,
are too far away from her for her to see. When the Judge
rejects her view, she refuses to affirm his action.
Her opinion is hardly quotable.

GENESIS

From nowhere known
it arrives. You try to coax it
to come to you; you feed it.

You give up, try to leave it,
but like a puppy,
it comes after you
and follows you around
and around, liking the game.

Or sometimes you throw
it about in some recently lit
corner of your mind
that could blacken
suddenly like a tennis court
somebody else put
the quarters in for.

It could hit you
just after black strikes.
Maybe you'll crawl in the dark
hoping to find it.
Before you hate yourself
for losing it, for giving up.

GOOD DAYS

Today
we have lived
in the same house
for twenty years. Married
for thirty-two. Our sons
are kind, confident, analytical.
Two are doctors. The third
is finishing his first year
of medical school.

Tomorrow
I intend to purchase
two or three packages or sets
or however they come now
of toy soldiers, the best
I can find, and a B-B gun.
I will place the soldiers
under the big tree
in the back yard,
some on bricks,
some partly hidden
in the grass, and shoot
at them from the garage
until I knock them all down.

HARD TIMES

Times and things were hard
in my home town in 1963.
To make the drag, less of one,
you sometimes had to steal a little
gas. We carried hoses.
The trick was not to swallow,
which gave us all a better feeling
for Melba Jean.

SECOND TOUR

When he was ten or so, he went to football practices
to watch and learn. His Dad took the car to work.
The son never had a bike. How did he get there?
The stands were often not full, but the important men
were always together, pointing to the field, smiling.

When he played *Eubanks and Hern* gave him a pair of shoes.
In the drug store he had his own cup. It was never empty.

He came home from college one weekend. The bus station
was full. His Dad told him all the people at church asked about him.

After war, he came home. Mrs. Jefferson nodded. I.B. Cupp
waved from across the street. At church, polite, cordial smiles
and many frowns. He polished his shoes, pinned ribbons back on,
hugged, kissed his red-eyed mother, shook his pale father's spotted hand.
His Dad drove him to an early plane to San Diego. He felt at home
going through Pendelton's main gate, but wondered how he got there.

How Are You So Good to See You What have You Been Doing?

In shadow light that obscures years,
we lean on elbows.
I try not to look down her blouse, fail.
My jaw hangs open.

As I catch a whiff of my '49 Ford,
gear shift cleverly placed on the left of the steering column,
I recall: white socks, two-tone oxfords,
a wide pink skirt with a poodle on the pocket,
a pony tail: her chewing gum so loud
you couldn't hear Johnny Ray's
clatter about crying clouds:
car radios blasting melting bodies
before conditioned air:
blankets to keep cockleburs from pricking us,
six packs of long-necker Pearl,
growing so
hot only two are consumed.

Where's your husband?
Busy tonight? Always busy?
The second husband was a prince.

How are the kids? Grandchildren?
Daughter married a mechanic
this time. The first time she was too young.
The grandkids are fine
with their fathers.

I know how kids are.
Where's my wife? At a far table,
glaring at her drink in my hand,
melting the ice.

The old girl places her hand
over her dangling bosom; I brace myself:
forget '49 Fords, hot beer on itching blankets.
"Be Good," I mumble.
She doesn't smile, looks off, hand clutching at her breast.

REQUIESCAT IN PACE

To my sons

You almost never remembered birthdays, so
try hard to mark and notice the annual day
of my death. You could ring bells, sound sirens, and go
about with short faces. Be sure to pay
the priest again and please joyfully embrace
my mistress who gave herself with hope—
a cheerful giver. Wipe tears from her wrong face
and if you should pass by the place the Pope
would put his emissary, please pray for her
without the woeful sorriest of sounds:
the organ that booms and blows to warn, a burr
within the ear of man that scares and pounds
the message home: another sinner's gone.
When you reflect on my request, don't moan.

Incalculable

Is virtue your faith? And me, is love my sin?
Because I love and cannot help myself,
Must I conclude the fault is deep within
My genes? Or can I blame some capricious elf?
But you, are you so certain you're on the path
Of God's own plan that you can throw us away?
You calculate your answers in God's math,
But are numbers known—insight by damned old clay?
Not many days are left for us to seize.
But there is no doubt for any; the best is yet
Not free. We'll pay. Don't care if we displease
The fates; the infinite fine scheme is set
Per Diem. Discount the charges for fustian fun,
And know our journey goes beyond the sun.

Keeping Up

Spring vacation was a cheap week
above the beach, avoiding a tan.
On the fourth floor above sweaty,
nearly nude volleyball players,
I lunged against determined servings
the whole time, pushing up six days.
On the seventh, I rested, stuck
my face out, trying to gather some sun,
made the best I could of an interlude
buried in the dark.

I carried her number,
new, unused for a year.
When I called,
her mother told me she had married,
thrown herself away
on a worthless beach bum.

KISSING HER

Not a nice image, perhaps
but the best way is to say
kissing her draws my breath
out of me
like one of those suction
things dentists use. I gasp.

My feelings, whatever they are,
tangled, pushing and pulling,
like braces forced into a place
not meant for such straightening,
not possible to make right.
The orthodontist is mad.

As I place my hand on her breast,
drilling through buttons,
slipping, anesthetized, under
covers of silk with cotton
padding my cheek, I never consider cost.

No real repair possible,
I think of Grandfather's teeth
in a jar by his open mouth,
looking as if they dare him
to put them in so they can bite
the snore out of him.

LINES COMPOSED THIRTY-EIGHT THOUSAND FEET ABOVE PHOENIX, JULY 13, 2006

"As democracy is perfected, the office of the president
represents more and more clearly, the inner soul of the
people. On some great and glorious day the plain folk of the
land will reach their heart's desire at last and The White
House will be adorned by a downright moron."
        H.L. Mencken (1880—1956)

Just me and hoards of others and my laptop squirting along
coach fashion in a pressurized tube, seeking Los Angeles
and my second son's cooler clime. I am unable to see Phoenix
arising, but if anybody is just waking or starting a fire

at noon in July, and I'm sure somebody is, I have no idea why.
The world is not much with me up here, little I can see of Nature,
from this unearthly height, not even a sordid sonic boom
can bare its bosom, whatever that means, or make its way

from here because of too much slow hot air, slightly lower.
The baby boomers and I are up-gathered like commuters
or any travelers out of tune above an unpleasant lea, and earth
has nothing more unfair to show than Iraq, Afghanistan,

and Geo II stuttering, grasping for thought, holding furiously
to lies and immense bad sense. Ten thousand of his untruths,
and all that mediocre heart lie-ing still on the muted screen
in front of me. One could not but be more morose in his company.

LOVE SONG

When one of the brothers
was pinned, my fraternity
serenaded her sorority.
I noted carefree singing
of love songs. I thought we lied
to one another, to one other.

Our chords struck sympathetic
overtones in the tower bells.

God willed a seraphim
singing angelic hymns
for my harmony.
Her golden, layered hair
flowed about my throat
strangling dissonant sounds.

More luscious than celestial wine,
softer than suspicions,
she was more desirable
than the Grail, than the cloistered letter jacket
a preppie had to be too cool to wear.

The coat clung to her
one ephemeral night, covering then undoing
doubts of phantasmal choirs.

Twenty years later the hallowed coat
is as new and attractive as original sin.
Sometimes I feverishly stick my nose
between buttons, catch a whiff
of the old stupefying incense.
I rub my face in Angel dust
until her halo glows. An infinity
later, in the shower, I sing timeless tunes.

THE MISS MELLOWTONES

Sometimes Joannie Kate went sharp
as her high, pushed up in a prom dress, breasts.
Miss Franklyn cringed briefly as though fingernails
had scraped the chalkboard from end to end.
Her face straightened, and she smiled
a pretty, vulnerable smile.
Joannie Kate could have been flat
as Miss Franklyn's chest, and I would have smiled.

Miss Franklyn sang beautifully and trilled
the notes back and forth, never missing one,
but she had no bosom and no boyfiend.
She had a picture of a red-headed young man,
who didn't know he had been preserved by film,
leaning on a car, looking toward mountains.
He was killed coming over a sharp rising hill
where an eighteen wheeler flattened him,
straightening a curve.
Miss F said her life sunk after that.

Joannie K and I crawled under the fence
where a dog had dug the original hole, into
the bus barn and climbed into
the long, uninterrupted bumpy back seat
and drank the three or four beers
she stole from her dad's garage refrigerator.
High on beer, adrenaline, and hormones,
we became a duet, doublebacked.

While Miss F patiently waited for the second coming
of Mr. Right, she was high on music.
In the deep dark of the back of the bus,
coming home from a choir trip
Joannie K and I too much anticipated
later doings until Miss F stood over us
and cried we were a disgrace to God, our school,
the choir, and The Mellowtones. I shriveled low

in the seat, but Joannie K stood in the aisle
and said that she didn't believe the red-headed guy,
leaning on the car, died. He ran

from a no-breasted warbler with skinny legs,
Joannie K said. Miss F said Joannie K
was no longer one fourth of The Mellowtones
because she was always sharp or flat.
Miss F cried all the way to the Principal's Office
the next day and Joannie K was no longer
in the choir; I was a hero. Miss F resigned,
took her picture of red hair and drove away.
Jamie Sue, a former Mellowtone with breasts
lowered three inches by ten years and two kids,
told me at the reunion that no one cared but me.
High and low, sharp and flat I loved them both,
she said impatiently.

OCTOBER SONG

Young bosoms bursting
through thin, loose-weave blouses,
tan legs beneath black shorts,
bare bellies flat out
make a man
whimper, mourn cool,
love summer.

Bare legs bicycling
through Spring
pump warmth
even into Fall.

Her red lips round
to greet ground ice.
She scoops her eyes
up at me and sucks
red juice into the corners
of her delicious mouth.

On a Pedestal

We run to them like they are our mothers
who pretend to listen to sand pile dreams.
We know they turned deaf as God after we made them
assume old poses. They wait to be rung out
on the ladder of success, worry, wonder if the hard
climb will be worth their time, decide other artists
are no better. Not much for them to do
but wait, pose occasionally, watch paint dry,
loosen their muscles, joints, inspect, clean
the finish. They cling to us, tell us what they want
to believe, together we will fetch a good price.
Their fingers curl around the brush,
squeeze out the hardening paint. We want
a model to know before the surface dries.

POSTURING

Most people shake their heads no
with ever decreasing arcs.
I like the lessening sweep of the head,
the pendulum of no,
slowing until the head is straight
as no one's virtue. A person is encouraged
by vacillations, especially if the head
drops its eyes, looking for a way
to hide the soul, but you look me straight,
never quavering,
shake your head once each way.

Most people have scoliosis of the skull,
deciding yes, no. Not you.
I wish the patio hedges
to be straight as your vertebrae.
No doubts creep up to be clipped off
like errant stems, popping-eager
to feel the soft tissue of leaves.

QUIZ

She sits in front of me
her legs cross into X.
Her breasts are full circles.
I pretend to read
then look past her
to the back rows.
Slowly my eyes come
forward to fantasy.
She rises
comes to me
seeking affirmation.
I say,
"yes, it's true."
Nodding, satisfied
she returns to continue
sorting fact from fiction.

Redact: Hail and Farewell

After Alfred missed his day in the sun,
Value, which he knew would run,
Emptied from his bald spot, burned, overdone

And looked for new lodgings
To secure itself in again, folding
Quaint newly rolled-up pant cuffs, holding
Undulating dandruff-like thought-puffs of dusting,
Enervating those who once were possessing

Vigor enough to eat peaches and play
Along rolling beaches, strolling away
Languidly toward an endless dark day
Eclipsed by long twirling skirts holding sway.

Repose

Stacy Barret came to me
out of a tunnel of darkness,
the beauty of the night,
professor of position, counter position.

After, I slept in her impression
warmed with remembrances:
sighs that lovers love,
perfume, bath oil, and her purr
blended in my repose.

Where's Stacy now,
buried in the dark?

My sheets are crisp and smell
of bleach and detergent. I have trouble
sleeping and often dream.

Robert E. Lee Park

That soul of honor, Robert E. Lee, is astride
his Traveller in the park. A man's empty eyes,
captured by Lee, absorbed his hours
while waiting for the Lady writer
from New York from long ago. She found life
halting in a conventional way and was in town
till noon Sunday. They stood where they lay
thirty years before and talked of old knights.
Nothing comes from such talk, bare talk.
The General's shadow didn't fall as the day
leaned toward a cloudy night. Then he was alone
and level headed, thinking about time, sands,
and dust, old visages. He stretched no boundaries
to put his hand on a knee, cold and bronze.

ADAM'S FAULT

What were they mad about? That
suspicious lot who fell like shaken salt
from the boat at Plymouth then began
to punish Jesus. I was introduced to Jesus,
thought Him unbelievable until mother
proved and reproved misunderstandings,
telling the church fathers she found
what I wanted, needed, gave it to me.
Godly gifts. The Plymouth crowd demanded,
but offered little freedom or forgiveness
or compassion. They earned, they said,
that which had been offered free, mother said.

SLIDING DOWN SLOPING CEMENT
FAR FROM HOME

We came home from separate colleges after our freshman
year. Began where we had left 9 months before.
She spent her summer days with a French tutor and a piano
teacher. I lifted 100 pound bags of cement from box cars, put
them in 18 wheelers. I drove home in 5 o'clock traffic,
had dinner with mother, showered, chose clothes
for the night and next day, drove 20 miles or so to her
front gate with guards. Up the only driveway I had ever seen
with speed limit signs (15 MPH) to her house. We walked
to her pool, the first private pool I had ever seen. It was
not large, but circular with no diving board. The pool
was a hundred yards precisely from the house but hidden
by a horseshoe hedge. We changed in the bath houses, played
5 or 6 33 & 1/3s then turned them over. Mostly Broadway tunes
from shows she had driven down to see. I wearied of them.

            It was all so uneven
I could almost walk to the center of the sloping pool, swim 3 strokes,
walk to the other edge to hold on again. I slept in a bedroom
far from hers, awakened early, drove to the guards and to work.
And we did it all again. And again, 3 summers.
The pool moved indoors one last Christmas, next to the house. Alas

Senior summer she came home and married
a Jewish boy who was shorter than she. A Harvard
man. A 10 o'clock wedding, I was not invited.
Couldn't afford the tall hat and the split tails anyway.
She knew. I sent a small package of powdered cement.
I'm not sure why.

Twenty years later she came to a poetry reading
I gave. Spoke to me after, returned the cement.
Glad to see her, we talked about mutual friends
who all did so well. She "resided" lived in Colorado Springs
and Dallas. All I remember, except she looked good.

About ten years later I heard she was a widow.
I googled her. She owned thousands of acres,
was on the board of many corporations.
I sent her a new brick-sized box of cement from my office
at the university. No card. The kind of cement powder
I breathed, washed off every day for 3 summers before
driving 20 miles to stand around the slippery edge of tepid water.

Stunning

Her hair was dark, almost black,
appeared smooth, soft.
The perfect hair was not long
unless you think to the shoulder
is long. The hair gently covered
her slightly rounded shoulders, stayed together,
each strand loving the other.
The shoulders, when she talked,
tried to meet in front of her words
as if they were forming a wave.
A soft downy breath uttered pure, distinct syllables
that hesitated to leave a pink, round mouth.

Words can do nothing
for features. Symmetrical,
neither side of her face ascendant.
Her eyes needed no help,
but if she had worn glasses
they would have been straight
as virtue across her face. Her waist
indented flatly, her hips sufficient
to support all eyes descending
to do her homage. The legs
under all pulchritude
were symmetrical as her face,
smooth as her hair, held her
about 5'7" above a fortunate floor.

When anyone, professors included,
didn't stare, he was pretending to be cool.
Eyes yearned to follow, to leave
a recalcitrant head that wouldn't bend or twist.

Jackie D'Ellis was, perhaps still is, the name
for a rare, fortuitous blend of genes
that did not return to SMU
for a second year.
The buildings mourned with doors hanging open,
windows weeping dust.

THE BORDER

When a person has nothing more to say
or worse, nothing more to think,
he should drive far unto the brink
of thought, say...Iowa.

Motor through familiar lands
and see the comfortable
farms and well developed plans.
Note a warping red gable
and high unending cloud-filled skies.
Pass through flat lands until you see
the end—an old state with no guard.
Then turn to home and tell no lies
about an easy relaxing journey,
and hold the vision in high regard.

BETWEEN GOOD AND BAD

My television darkens then lightens,
and I don't want to leave my bed
and do anything. Doing is dangerous
and often boring at the same time.

I want to see others and be pulled into their
lives like a genie slipping, all exhausted,
back into his bottle. I promise if I don't
have to get up even for the bathroom, I will root

for the good guys, most of the time.
If though, Clint Eastwood is a bad guy
I may root for him anyway. I don't know why,
but I also don't know why I often read,

"Empedocles on Etna." It defies all I know
of good, evil, and tragedy. Empedocles jumping
is no tragedy, but sad. All of the good guys must fall,
but so do all the bad guys. I know I love Claudius

as he prays, and only in the old Saturday matinees
is the situation clear. Something about the color
of horses and hats is simple enough for me.
I also admit that I love Iago. Time and I worship

language and forgive everyone by whom it lives.
Polonious perpend, I love you too.

THE MAYOR

Would you be the Mayor
of Cisco, Tx—a town full
of Rottweilers and Pit Bulls
with nothing to guard? You know
the word moribund? Cisco
is mostabund. A bad joke,
Cisco, but the Mayor—
what is he to do? Nights he hears
Ft. Worth/El Paso pulsing by
on the interstate. He sees the town,
his florist shop, decaying.
Wal-Mart snubs him.
No McDonald's, and a tornado
brushed away the Dairy Queen
like broken glass in a dust pan.
No plans to rebuild.
The street lights dim.

THE NERVE OF SOME PEOPLE

Playing blackjack in Vegas,
my backbone collapses
as the man next to me complains
I don't know when to hit.
I've somehow changed his luck.
How does he know
what the next twenty cards will bring?
One card off now may be luck later.
The difference betwixt a benefit
and an injury: who can tell?

My friend tells me
that because I had my heart opened
antioxidants did me no good.
How does he know
when I might have died
if I hadn't taken them?

The only way to see the future
is to travel
in time with Jim and Spock,
watch God maneuver.

Oh Science Fiction, sweetheart,
let us in on God's plan.
Is the Nostradamass
next to me gonna be hit
by a train
or does the world make no sense?

THE OVERTURE

I hear your other song,
you fever-spreading siren
of another stage.

Your large eyes half-hidden
by sullen lids, your thin breasts
framed by long, smooth blonde hair,
round out above thin hips that support jeans,
sagging in the center, slightly beneath your navel.
You are always barefooted
in a bronze Sophie Newcomb shirt
with blue letters,
leaning in several poses against pure white pillars.

In dim restaurants, boxes
at the theater, anywhere,
you hum breathy strong notes
in concert as I wrap my hand
in the householder's fretting fingers.
Looking upward, I shake my head
clear of the touch of dissonance.

THE RING OF KAPPA ALPHA ORDER

For DB

Though I would push the frat away, it holds
and clings, until scars remain embedded in
my thoughts, refusing to grow decrepit, just old.
The wonder-grasp on me has grown so strong
that my spotted hand has aged around a pen,
scratching for reasons to explain a claim long
endured deep throughout my psyche within
a shining, infinite ring of ten caret gold.
Why should I write? No reason but peace from art—
a mere sleight of hand, designed to confound
a belief that brotherhood could start
on lack-brain theories of eternal friends.
Among a tribe of erudites, the shaman's
duties are thought to be the will of the clan.

TO A DEAD FAT COMEDIAN/ACTOR

His eyes were never bigger than his brunch.
Against his will, he'd eat, increase his span
And blow his blow-fish body like a punch
In the solar plexus after a large lunch.
So big a clown as ever broke his divan,
He made some fun, not love. What else to do
When one is trapped inside his vest but expand?
The extended plan became too big for man—
No life within the swollen blimp askew

His act to find a woman? Not interested.
He could not find one for his personal crew.
Too huge for love, he searched for life off cue.

What came of all those jokes he ingested?
Some hardy laughs and cash, but love—divested.

GRACE

You taught me how to catch and punt footballs,
to shoot pool, to play poker. When games carried songs,
smiles, I learned not to suffer long from falls.

We measured all the distance for all the little balls,
and big. We calculated wind, weight, pawns,
rooks, kings though not of the great halls.
Some boys learned carpentry, then mechanics.
My sorrow-kit for their lack of time on lawns
was firmly full as bulging picnic baskets.

A boy should learn importance from his father.
I learned all there is to know about balance,
speed, thought, talk. What else to know of love or

leaping in fray could possibly be better?
You thought you never taught for fame or palace,
but in that concern you were wrong. Never bitter

about what you didn't have to give, I gathered
all that springs to birth from the many pleasured
earth. What you provided is all treasure.
To be with you was delight in full measure.

Unplanned Obsolescing

In the late fall when a man reaches
for the lawnmower in his garage,
he grasps a tilted baseball bat,
breathes faster,
hoping for a high hard one.

The pipes under his leaking sink
squeal a little like the lady VP
who won't touch messy Xerox parts.

When a middle management man
leaves his wife
every morning
he loves a minute
with a creamy-skinned secretary
generously massaging the coffee machine
as she pours rich, hot, striking substance
into his creamy cup.

VARIATION ON A THEME BY FRANK O'HARA

The Jackson One

Michael Jackson has collapsed!
He was cavorting and no doubt
contorting, and we didn't know
he was dehydrated (contorting
is difficult for a body) and
his electrolytes were off. Well,
truth to tell, we knew something
was off. My friend Dick said he
thought it was Michael's nose.
No doubt Michael put his nose
somewhere he shouldn't, but
that wouldn't make him collapse,
would it? Oh, I have made gatherings
and acted actually awful, but I never
came close to collapse. My nose
was not out of joint or in one.
Oh Michael we love you. Get up,
get up! There is heavy snow
in Hollywood, and the sun does
not shine in Joyland, or is it
Never Netherland? Whatnever.
Could you have Liz tell us
when you are up and about again?
Boy!   Talk about sad!

VINEYARDS

When strolling through poetry arbors,
hoping to come upon
certain shimmering lines
that your good taste
demands. I select succulent,
ripe verse parts, gleaming
like my desire
to swallow you
immersed in the ardor
of vivid, heady wines.

WHEN PRESSED

For Jim, the Family Felon

Who can calculate how much paper
you misplaced: deeds, notes receivable?
Your losses are heavy as the unused cold air
of your lost sauna, also mortgaged twice. A hot cell

will compensate. What do you think about
today? What weighs on you: the box
with conditioned air at Texas Stadium?
A cherished blue parking pass close to a dome,

ringed with names that reverberate glory?
Landry, Staubach, guys you said you loved,
never filched good names. Yours, you
lightly sailed away like a hat in an arena.

That membership at Los Colinas was hefty
as the gothic bag of clubs you used to big shot
around like a tee shot by a Tiger. Yeah,
you pranced, fat cat. Maybe the Rotary Club

where you strutted, but now stand in memory
like a broken spoke, is oppressive: You wobbling
wheeler-dealer, out-of-balance, cursed phony.
I, Teiresas, your former family caddy,

warned the tribe not to take pride in you.
I counted strokes, listening to the wind.

WHISPERS

Joannie Kate sang in the choir
because I did. Everyone knew.
She was tall, slim, wore glasses
and had an hour-glass figure
below a face long as six o'clock.
On choir trips after dark
she put herself in my hands.
Late hours we met in the bus barn
where she would whisper my name.

In the light of days, I knew
no time for her, but the dark
of the moon heard her breath
upon me, as I drifted like sand
to her, this first girl who wanted me.

Later, she gracefully directed
singers of timeless music
at the high school, married a mortician,
and died of breast cancer.
Breath-filled arpeggios from sibilant
youths should have protected her.

When she slid beyond sound,
beyond measured beats,
I sent a requiem mass
of wavering bouquets—
perennials—
to the bus barn.

Always in my view
one violet lies
by the bus-barn wall
with light moth wing shadows
fanning its petals.

The sun stands still for her;
I hear her breathe my name
when the wind, moon rise.

WINDSWEPT

The waves pounded the shore
as she lovingly vowed never
to leave me alone when wind
pushes heavy, white surf.

She came with soggy old baggage,
carrying memories inconveniently arranged.
She floated with her head
back, looking for formations to rearrange

in a cloudy dark sky. She struck out,
plunging in deep troughs
toward the rough deep, then came back
riding the wild water, balanced with regret.

The groaning wind tried to warn
me, but the water roared.

WILL

A Lot You'd Care

The word according to John gunned me down
before I learned to duck, shoot back. Rising
like a zombie from my seat, ambling cockily
in front of my reflection in the mirror

behind the candy, right hand slightly lower,
I vowed to be a straight shooter
like John. His actions and some of his words,
listen to *The Shootist*, where he revealed his code

not to treat people badly, said he wouldn't allow
himself to be treated like Job. His ordinary remedies
for folk: a simple doctrine, with a sympathetic tone,
resonated through my un-stretched vocal cords.

He spilled over the edge of my life like bulging
popcorn boxes, squeezed hard. But what if a blackhatted
six-foot-thirteen agile villain, eager to sacrifice
with my blood, a guy bigger than an NFL lineman,

quicker than a fourteen year-old sinking in
passion's first storm, came for you and me, John?
I behold you tip-toeing past him like Peter saying,
"Not me, no sir." What cocky words would you crow

then? Looking back during reflection time, above
the candy and popcorn, I see you
like Ritchie slinking away from an angry Fonze.
Where do those windy paths of glory go, Marrion?

They lead to the toilette till the maelstrom passes,
swirling laughter like a winner at roulette.
I mouth your words with kernels stuck
in my throat behind mounds and mounds of salt.

After Miriam, My Sister

After Miriam died and her boys were gone
to live with their father, Dad drank by himself.
Just beer, but he often threw up on the lawn.
The pantry that Mom filled on every shelf
with rice and beans and more nutritious stuff
was now a habitat for cans of Bud.
Dad's neighbor, a friend as wise as Odysseus,
called me from time to time to tell of blood
in father's effluence. It stained the grass.
Straighter than sin I would arrive at his house
and argue him to doctors and to Mass.
No talk would ease his pain. He'd make no vows;
neither priest nor doctor could control his fever.
Miriam did not survive the ether.

ALL AT SEA

In Memoriam L.M.R. 1908-1992

Mother's calm becalmed my wayward accusers.
Her cool demeanor, not always her behavior,
forced a foaming, untidy response from the churchmen.
Uncoiling like Thetis from the water,
she said, "I learn his wants. If it's no sin,
I get it for him." Islands of stranded pain,
like marooned seamen signaling in vain,
their prelatical faces fell in clerical splatter.
They wavered beside the baptism font, defeated.
Indolent as lazy waves sweeping seaward,
I steered her slowly from their dried up clatter.
At the altar rail she kneeled and whispered,
"Thank you son. You remind me of your father.
He was an iconoclast and no good either."

ALLURE

When I water the lawn, birds appear
instantly. Do they have timers?
Do they have scouts aloft?
Are they the same birds?
Once I loved mystery, now I wish
for unpredictable pleasure after flying
high, desiring to wing water over my head,
fly away when whim dictates.

My daughter-in-law moved on.
She always flitted about like some little bird
locked out of its cage, looking frantically
for some way out, flying from one curtain rod
to another, bumping its head on windows.

My divorced son vacationed in San Francisco
then moved there. He can
doctor anywhere. Texas is sin hot,
but why so far? Is it the cool salt air
pushing predictable tides, allowing birds
to remain aloft without fluttering wings?

AN ANNUAL SOLUTION

Never raised his hand or voice to me
and when a man doesn't say much, you tend
to listen. My father would pull me aside
and force instruction on me like dictation.
Damned if he didn't feel compelled to help
nature. When he decided winter was over,
no matter the calendar, selection was made
and any animal who was shaggy or too close
was sheared. Horses had to look good for father—
a trader. They stood, fetlock deep, in shorn
hair and would crowd one against the other,
hiding, warding off shame and cold.
I remember them, always, like grainy black
and white film of Jews, naked, hairless,
covering private parts with their hands
as they were shot. Some last indignity,
herded together, hairless. I pulled
my Stetson down snug, never doubting
father's final wisdom.

AN EMPTY STADIUM: THE EVE OF ASTROTURF

For Ryan, my grandson

The dust dredged up forty years
ago by cleated feet drifts down
to cloud sacrifice, threatens
conversion. Only yards from the goal,
a midnight fire releases ashes
of yellowed clippings, wafting through
thin echoes, thick clouds to futile gods.

No longer preserved by troubadours,
pagan fame rises in smoke,
seeking something to nourish.

"BLACK AS THE PIT...."

Like a shadow racing toward night,
the blackened stack of the barbecue pit
climbed the back fence.

My father spent his day by pit, pool.
Late afternoon I left, returned
after dark, caught the scent of fear
pulling like a waterfall.
Dad, inching his way by the diving board,
cursed the night that had covered him.

Right ankle bent like lost virtue, he wanted
bourbon before the hospital's sterile solace.

Wrestled like conscience
into a checkered deck chair,
he panted his confession:
he had scaled the smutty stack
of the pit to reach
for the waiting woman
in the black, wooded yard next door.
Her husband home, Dad groped in darkness,
lost direction, fell.

He leaned to the water, eased in,
absolved himself with bourbon, chlorine.

Years later I helped the old man
cane his way to the car at the cemetery.
Holding a thorny rose from mother's casket,
he said, "About that night,
wasn't worth it. She smelled
of onions." I held one laugh down
a winding path.

Unconquerable, he was.

BURNING

Your neighbors never know you're a poet.
your parents worry, your children
count their toes, embarrassed.

At the family reunion, Uncle Orville,
the rich one with the young, pretty wife,
laughs at your parents, ignores your children

talks, brags about his deals, not too slyly.
When the conversation turns from him,
In white hot sun, he proclaims,

a poet! By God, how's he make a living?
Mother pales, father reddens, stammers,
"teaching." Miriam, the pretty young wife, smiles

with her thighs, bends, brushes a fly off
her narrow ankle, offers me a breast.
Her eyes are a picnic. She asks me for something

to read, says she loves what I do. She
doesn't understand much, but Uncle Orville
turning from pale to glaring red, does.

CLARITY

"Are not two sparrows sold for a penny?
yet not one of them will fall to the ground
apart from the will of your father." Matt. 10: 29

I admit that years ago I began to bribe
the blue jays, mockingbirds, and red birds that live
or often visit in my back yard. I rarely see sparrows.

My yard is secluded and has many trees.
I have put running water on both sides of the patio
that is surrounded by large oaks.

The point here is not to describe the beauty of my yard,
but rather to try to understand and perhaps explain
why some four or five times in the last 33 years

I have had to have funerals for sparrows that fly
into my bay window which has no curtains or shades.
I have found sparrows dead on the patio before,

but this one I heard hit the window. I take
that sound with me now. It flies with me
on my way to town or even to other rooms.

I saw this bird a few seconds after it hit. It was lying neatly
with its wings folded. It had no position of death.
I thought it might shake its head, think what a fine

head-thumping nap he had and fly away to be
as he had been. Even his feet were tucked away
as if in flight. There was no blood, no bent neck

of death. And no movement. I sprinkle seed generously
all over the patio so as to avoid disputes, but I know
I almost never see sparrows. Have the larger, prettier

more eloquent birds claimed my yard for their own?
I have no notion how to make them share. Maybe birds
can't see the results of their actions, either. Maybe some

sparrows fall from the sky for a few pecks, a few sips,
then zip away, but the speed that kills must take longer
to achieve than a quick start can give. No longer

can I wonder if I am a contributor. I must put on my white
gloves, pick up the remains, so perfect they seem
and stroll to the place by the stock tank

where I frequently find remains of coyote-strewn
rabbit carcasses. I place the bird close to a cactus
kick some leaves on it and leave nature to its way.

My nephew a Marine Lt. Colonel now in Iraq could not
have seen where he was headed when he entered
the Naval Academy nineteen years ago. I remember

he had perfect pictures of nobility, such a clear path.
I admit now the need for plantation shutters.

CONSTANCE

Rivers empty into clouds;
the sun sucks energy from plants;
trains refuse their tracks; elevator music isn't loud,
except their songs for you. Windows weep dust;
the tides push moons away; things galvanized rust.
The three tenors lower their voices, drop their pants:
Doors hang open, hoping you'll walk through.
as I do, thinking of and loving you.

The mountains bow to forests;
the sun cools my brow.
The Marine Corps makes boys;
sailors are not on the prowl.
Our sons refuse dessert, ignore toys;
Snow White sings the blues off key,
beats a darling, sweet Queen to mirrors, sees
the forward way I love you.

Mother Teresea hates the sinner,
loves sin. Broadway converts to heterosexuality.
Indians pollute the earth, sky, sea.
Anyone can guess who's coming to dinner.
Sidney Poitier raps; Pulver becomes a winner.
John McCain loves his guarders,
decides to come home out of order.
Custer retreats, but I continue loving you.

Dick Clark ages; Betty Grable acts.
John Cleese makes dead parrots talk.
Coke comes along with a classic view.
Ford makes Edsel. Jacque Tati talks.
Poker-faced Marcel Marceau stalks
French women, shaves their underarms.
New math changes. Quantas takes short walks
beneath alluvian shores. Looking up, I love you.

Baseball bats breed, beat on trees. Sam Donaldson,
Cokie Roberts sound pundit alarms.
Rudy Valentino, Errol Flynn learn Richard Gere.
Bill Clements talks straight; SMU has a good year.
San Francisco breaks a Golden Gate.
LA is deserted. Long Beach shortens.
Commuters are never on the run.
Arabs, Jews, Irish, Turks, and Greeks call off hate.
Greenwich time is always late.
Theaters never open, shut curtains,
but I act, and always, all ways love you.

Cynthia's Reflection

I turn out the small lamp
beside my bed and walk
to the window to see the light
drawn out and up. But I know
the moon gathers my energy
to spread on lovers like my son
who, two hundred miles from home
at my old college, is at this moment,
I hope, in his car with some young lovely
who reminds me of his mother
now breathing softly, waiting
for me to come to her
before all our light is gone.

DRY

As we dug the holes to bury the bois d' arc posts,
we agreed that never again we'd repeat the chore:
a fence to keep domestics in, beasts out.

The sweaty scar on his cheek glistened moist
when digging and injecting controlling order
in or on his place. His life was about

teaching success without a hint of gloat
like a Roman's slave, he whispered as he bore
the burden of wire and wood: "Fame is bought."

Standing on his spade, removing a coat
of rock-covered clay, he'd look for more
to lift, to remind me of human drought.

If I didn't note his earth sermons, he'd pout.
A baptism by sweat, required to be devout.

Empty Nest

He hears "Daddy," in the wind;
the pickup slides in at *Athletic Supply*
where gloves, balls, fondle hands,
screaming high ones hidden behind his eyes.

Home, he strikes out to mend
a perfect fence, stares at a swollen mare.
Who will smile at a stumbling foal's slick hair?
Young city men have little time.

Around the house, pool cues bend
as tilted, signed, baseball bats blend
in hot corners, no longer wary
of sweating palms, curving signs.

She cooks to the year's end;
he stokes the fire, reclines unaware
of short passes that fly by his chair;
high punts glide over him in waves

of abstracted air. He sends soft sleep moans
to muted saxophones resisting blare;
she turns the TV cheers low, saves
numbers for new cell phones.

He always knew sports, remembers
exciting falls embedded in searing embers,
rooting for Tommy Nobis,
and Johnny Unitas.

ENTRANCED

I strapped golden time
on your wrist, forced
a shimmering cross between your breasts,
wrapped your long slender finger
with gold.

Weighted, you could not betray
your winsome stance,
but sway gently,
chime softly to my soul.

Your lulling music, dance
gives me power
to fend off dragon fire,
protect our poem bower.

FAMILY GET-TOGETHER

My cousin was my first.
She was fifteen. I, thirteen.
She is forty-five now,
and we have not spoken of our (?)
in thirty years. I think
about our (?) every Christmas
when the family gets together
to exchange gifts.

FAMILY TIES

An errand boy, I knocked softly on Aunt Gladys' door.
She was wearing high heels, hose, garter belt, a robe
open as a fifteen year old boy's face. Her bra,
panties, white as the Virgin's feet
in Saint Rita's Catholic Church.
Her lips redder than the barn
on the east edge of town
proclaiming
  Welcome
to Abilene.

She asked me in, her pale robe fell off her shoulders,
where her long black hair reformed immediately,
asked what I wanted, took my face
in her hands, kissed me
with her tongue.
I told her mother
wanted her,
Uncle Beau
  to come
to supper.

Aunt Gladys packed her brown imitation leather suitcase,
left in Uncle Beau's blue 59 Ford
two weeks later. No one
has seen her since.
I regretted my
thoughtless
  reaction
for years.

Future Perfect

For Connie

In some time
not far from now
I will have
always loved you.

GENERATIONS

Days of atonement—we might have been Jewish
except we were Episcopalian.
After Sunday lunch, mother started.
She vacuumed the tops of curtain arcs in rooms

with ceilings twelve feet high. Rooms none entered
unless they were almost strangers, no covenant
with them. Mother polished the glossy tops
of tables no one dared approach. Only she

possessed the secret of survivable touch.
Father paid his price beside the garage
with a chamois skin that could not be made dry.
One drop of holy water always remained.

Squeeze until the blood would run from your
wrinkled hand, there was always another drop.
If one water spot had continued in the Red Sea,
father would not have crossed. Grandfather did not

trust decadent, work-easing cars. If he had only
known what pleasures lay in automobiles,
he would have plowed them under. Moral
tractors: no pleasure there, except in an ethic.

I was naked after church, nowhere to hide,
like a hungry child, shown in black and white
pictures, starving in Europe, pursued by Devils.
Father was relentless in his desire for my
purification by soul-cleansing, hand-chapping,
wet-work, car cleaning. Sundays were eternal.
A sip of wine transferred father to a higher level
of hellish activity where he could guard
against an afternoon nap, even after
the heavy toll had been extracted. Some day
my sons will look back on Sundays, know
votive candles in front of blue screens

saved the Cowboys from relentless pursuit
by demons storming in from Philadelphia,
New York, Washington and other exotic, exile
places. Endless babble from pundits will tell
them they have been redeemed. They can relax,
watch crops grow, the sun return, devils depart.

Glaring

I'd like to snuff the sun for a moment,
drift in darkness like a lazy afternoon
shadow to watch you radiate a day,
playing bridge maybe, your golden fingers

snapping cards to unwary players, stroking
a small hairless dog's head, snuggling in your lap:
the daily things I have imagined for years.
I watch you in your robe, fetching, the morning

paper unraveling eagerly in your quick hands.
You stop traffic, turning heads toward your
beaming face, drawing attention like moths
growing inflamed. Morning flowers open

to bring your face. Insects crawl toward your wayward
ways. Birds warn, but I whistle along, blending praise.

GOOD NEWS

Aunt Mary popped from a coven of Methodists
like a drop of water in a pan of burning grease.
She married a tall Pentecostal preacher who saved her
for himself. The next time we saw her after she ran off,

her yellow hair was piled as high on her head
as her husband's stiff white collar
gleaming above his shiny black suit.
Mary, a little girl-woman, had grown large

with the Holy Spirit and child. Her sisters looked low
when the floor sweepings of Mary's homemade
summer dress cleaned the depths
of the cracks in the tent's wooden floor.

Mary, shy Mary, swept around her husband's tent
during meeting time, comforting the needy,
who had no greater need than to atone for sins
by giving of the fruits of their good works.

Her tender little voice pierced the penitent
through the depths of their thin wallets.
Doing the Lord's work made her strong she said.
Grandfather looked down, counting the eyelets

in his sturdy boots all though the service.
Grandmother clutched tissues every moment of endless
hymns. The sermon cleared her red eyes as she looked
to heaven. In the old car, rolling home in fear

of breaking down, Grandmother broke the quiet
saying she wished they had let Mary
date the Greenberg boy in high school.
Nobody nodded, but Grandfather sniffled,

maiden Aunt Anna sighed. Grandmother, seeing
herself in the window, said it would be nice to have purpose.

IMPRESSIONABLE

One part of me wonders how to impress the class
I grew toward the skies with. My growth is not as noticeable
as my lawn after a night of rain during days of drought.
Read my books, I say, and wish I had said nothing.

One part of me caught a pass deep in Texas territory,
and laughed drinking beer that night. The other me
remembers striking out with the bat on my shoulder,
continues to cringe at Ohhs and sighs.

Why is it that after reading many books, I am never
more than I am? One part can't convince the other
what is best—a hundred books or a hundred balls?
I give up. I'll never convince me I am more than a bug,
yearning to fly, to sting some former cheerleader's ass.

INCORPOREAL

My wife
likes to cuddle
without sex.
She wants to be
wanted.
She doesn't want me,
not for sex,
any way. I know
I'm different now,
forty years later.
I take too long
to do what once
I was too quick
for. You can't please
some people.
I'm considering
hiring a lay person.

LONGEVITY

Uncle Emmit died of a mad dog bite
at age nineteen. Fifty-year-old Uncle Fred
from a horse who fell backward and drove
a saddle horn through his chest. Uncle
Bob from a heart attack at age forty-two.
Uncle Wade was attacked by his heart
unto death at age fifty-nine. Cousin Ralph
lasted until he was forty-five—heart too.
I'm ahead of the game and feel like a winner,
but cousin Ike, who finished high school,
said he thought there was no point
in my having earned a doctorate if I had to die
too. I nodded slowly and sipped cautiously
another glass of cousin Ralph's homemade wine.

MAELSTROM AFTER SURGERY

Out of body is not bad.
Waking is terror, like the hood
dropped over your head
on the scaffold,
jerked off by the noose
as you fall into life.
The view rushes
as you ascend, expanding.
in a tunnel that leaves,
forgets you,
like your mother, waving good bye
in an offhand fashion.

Swirling space like a malevolent tornado
burst indifferently through
a dark room as it sweeps light
into a tiny glow
far above your reach.

Me Morning, Her June

I see you stretch the cover
tight over your turned shoulder.
A looser blanket might fool me,

but I know Spring is not here.
I can, must wait for warm
weather when some cycle sings.

I know—for children only,
only at night. You may loosen
your pull. Darling, be filled with care

your hand and more may turn
to salt if you look back over
that furious grip just under your hair.

MENTSH

For George Nilan, Bill Robinson, Frank Rieblin,
Del Saxon, Dick Bosse, Halton Henderson,
Bob Windham

The first professional Jew most of us
in our Christian fraternity knew was
Sam Tillinger. Sam owned the *Kilarney Bar*
and Lounge. I thought for years that *Killarney*

was spelled with one L because I was ignorant
and Sam was too close to his dollars to pay for the second
green neon L. Oh Sam, you knew. Your "Oy Vey!
You couldn't tip an old man a dime?" Brought you

a quarter every time. You were the attraction
we applauded. Lieberman disliked you,
wanted you spirited away,
kept quiet. You were his Jewish problem.

Your puffy fingers caressed quarters shiny
as your bald head and well-polished, nickel-plated
cash register keys. Your heavy-handed wife's
slitted eyes glared from the kitchen, pin spotting,

praising every performance, spurring you on
night after night until God stabbed you
in the chest like Lieberman's probing finger,
telling you you were too Jewish. *Kilarney*

has enough Ls. The five birthday dollars
you gave me for the date with the blond shicksa
earns interest for you. Rosary after Rosary winds
its way heavenward forty years later;

tree after tree grows in Israel for you.
The brotherhood and I toast you decade
after decade. Mazel tov! We hold
LLove for you eternally.

MOTHER SWINGING BY THE HOUSE

She described the feeling
as standing on the scaffold, hands tied,
the man in black dropping a hood over her head.

The next day she couldn't understand
why thousands of cars hurried.
She knew there was nowhere to go.

Some years she ate furiously to keep the blood
from her head. The next few years she ate nothing
for the same reason.

She moaned prayers almost all of every night,
attended meetings every thirty minutes
with persons who drank cokes, smelled of cigarettes.

Some facsimile came home occasionally,
smiled dully, asked who we were. We never knew.

NEOLITHIC

We moved the house years ago
back in woods where we can sit
on old carved stones from some lithic
age. Flashing faces from passing windows
can not see us there, looking deep
in humus for the old, our ties
to a past not denied by sighs.
We hear mother calling and creep
toward her voice like tendrils long left
with nothing to support. Brother sees
Poppa's head bobbing in walnut trees.
Miriam floats about bereft
of dances, beaux. We sing
her song, watch her wash with well water
until cars and other matters
of the present rush us to cling
to one another as we pet nieces,
nephews, gather life as it increases.

NO HUNTING

*"A mature jackrabbit eats as much grass as a cow and a
yearling calf."—A First Text on Agriculture, Goen Kibbling*

In Texas summers, the innumerable
long hot days radiate heat in observable
waves for hours before noon. When the sun
begins to slip, grass rises to meet the deer,

cattle, hide the nocturnal snakes. The lure
of silver water, sparkling fish bubbling
about the depths of life, calls evening visitors,
attracts a parade, stopping for a friendly drink

while the oval sun provides brief protection
minutes before the slanted moon slides
around with a knowing smile. Jackrabbits, somehow
believing in yesterday's conflation safety

in unbelievable sanctuaries begin
to cluster like old Marines in bars, drinking,
telling war stories. Slightly before the sun
looks away, jacks in increasing numbers

voraciously rip away a killing zone,
making land no animal's for a hundred
yards around a stock pond. Cattle must
be able to lower their heads, believe

they can wrap their pink tongues around long, green grass
forever as they graze, amble to water.
Coyotes, good accountants, watch carefully,
never doubt nature's faithful numbers.

NOT SO MUCH

When you look in the mirror,
you forget that in one step;
you're thirty-five again.

However it happens
women never flirt.

When you read *The Chronicle,*
realize nothing
applies to you, nothing
you are interested in
is interested in you,
then you know.

You stroll to the park,
rather than the library,
looking at the sky as if it were important.
No point in polishing
French.
No one
will discuss the subjunctive.

You sit in the park,
refuse to stare
at anything animate.
Dogs with shiny coats,
sporting silver tags that clink
to announce their arrival,
sense no desperation,
stroll on to sniff
something interesting,
far far away.

OF COURSE

I will tell them to be careful;
They will assure me with easy smiles.
I know they will do seventy-five
And more into the crowded terminal
For a tube that will hurl them toward
Phones at their hips or in deep pockets,
Supported indifferently by broad shoulders.
They will say what a good Thanksgiving
They had. I look through a dust-weeping window
To a chipped, scratched red table on a cracking,
Concrete patio where they stared barnward,
White-eyed at a snorting, dappled stallion
I broke, sold off this place where I grow drowsy

That horse

       Gone long ago.

Under Walden Tank

I woke up in San Francisco not long ago
where no one could walk a block without
being approached by a panhandler.

I worry about the homeless, do
little but dig deeper and give
more than I intend. Back home a cold
snap has hit.

I wish I could help myself not think
about the fish under the thick, opaque
slabs of ice, but chopping ice with an ax
is a pleasant job, unlike cutting off limbs

squeezing through, destroying fences.
Cattle must drink, and farmers-ranchers chop walls
of water every day until times are better,
until this time passes. A man can see

what he has accomplished chopping ice.
Taking care of the protruding limbs
is necessary, but no pleasure arises
watching stubs fall.

Under that murky ice, which fish fall
to become scavengers, bottom feeders?

ONE WIFE,

three sons,
two VCRs, two DVDs
two pickups,
three horses,
three hundred acres,
four hundred poems,
four computers
four TVs
five phones,
I missed something.

Only Thoughts Return to the Same True Places

We told the same stories all week and laughed
at the same places in the narrative as always.
Tonight we lie in four different beds
all bound to journey in different directions
while the world travels no known path.
The moon lights my wife for a few minutes
then shifts its focus, searching. She turns
sleeping, dreaming of her sons laughing.
Alarm sounds and vacation ends. She fails
to notice the moon receding, the slight
rising of the sun. The wind pushes the heavy
heads of grain toward us. Horses in the corral
calmly crowd one another, brushing away
annoyance coming in with the morning heat.
Sons ready to leave with their true wives.

ORATION

The first one to speak after making love says something
stupid. (old French expression, really)

I'm no good at speaking love;
My word flies too fast when feeling it.
My senses somehow rove
about betrayed: my tongue is split.

Wild words come scrambled, zooming out
which should no doubt have been concealed.
My brain may be in doubt
when words en route slide through congealed.

You must know or maybe think I'm dense
to sputter my soliloquy
and trample on fair sense.
I suffer from intensity.

In any vale or on any peak
I can claim love, albeit shrilly.
But the one who dares to speak
of love and flesh says something silly.

OUTLAW STORIES

He turned back watches, wall clocks, calendars
to lift bored, moody, wrinkled brows.
He'd tell intriguing stories to make hours
fall from work-filled view like furrowing plows.
He turned fancy-filled tales like scented earth:
rich, sweet-smelling, pleasure-promised birth
of bountiful ever-changing characters
buried in well-known, always verdant lots.
Up would pop some unknown actors
to perform old feats of freshly nurtured
actions within the common events. When he died,
my father said his father's use-worn old plots
were true but never happened. They vied
in Dad's misty eyes with myths never proscribed.

PAP

I did not know Pap well. He wasn't a friendly sort,
at least not with me, a city kid, according to him.
I lived just outside of Dallas, and he preferred
his grandchildren who lived on the ranch.
He was eighty-two and I was fifteen when he died.
I had cowboyed for him summers and Christmas
for years, never pleased him. That death day
my father and his brothers all remembered
when the well was at the back door. Some time later
when most of them had gone to the city, Pap put a pump
in the kitchen. His two daughters, unmarried twins,
squealed and invited the whole family to come see
the marvel. I remember. Finally, there was light,
electricity, in the house. Bare bulbs hung from high ceilings
on long thick cords.

Those nights before the funeral
my father and his brothers, some from cities,
took turns sitting with Pap in the parlor, which was lighted
only by two tall candles, one at each end of the casket.
Pap was wearing his dark blue city suit, and his long gray
hair seemed whiter. His hands were cold: his big diamond ring
glowed in the candle light. An old black man named Moon
came to pay his respects then all the brothers cried
and caressed the hair and hands.

PLAYING THE GAME

Red faced as the ranchers
we descended from,
my father and his brothers-in-law
played moon, forty-two, laughed
till glasses wobbled, measured manhood
by dealing. Mother and pale sisters gossiped
quietly, whispered ideas
as curtains rushed wind toward them,
fanning thoughts. Younger cousins,
invited to play, made money, dropped deals
like dominoes to the men.
I taught British literature,
sat silently in the kitchen with women
where the breeze was always sweeter.

PROSPECTORS

We searched our way some forty years or more
And on our journey noticed paths decay.
The tears that slid along, a flow of ore,
Were certain signs to show yet ease the way.
Just once we came across a small fissure;
Bulging pressure that helped to find the load.
That which we found was not in vein but pure.
The love that rose came slow as pans of gold.
If search must stop before our scores-plus years
Sluice past, as I suspect search always must,
Then know it was our labored love's desires
That made a golden thing of sinful dust.
If love falls not away from you and me,
The reason's not clear as love: It's alchemy.

Childish

A stoop-shouldered English professor
forced a senior out of registration,
made him go back about three hours
in the process because the student's trial study schedule
was not "neat." It was barely legible,
but such schedules are for the student only.
The student seethed.

One year later the new graduate student
was whistling his way to class
in a crowded hallway. The professor
came out of his office, remembered something,
set a leather briefcase with his brassy initials on it
by the open door to his office. A pretty sophomore
girl in a red dress followed him in and shut the door.

The usually timid student picked up the case
confidently, realizing that with every step
he was risking a life sentence in a gas station
or selling encyclopedias. He hurried out
the front entrance, delicately balanced
the case on the narrow concrete rail by the steps.
Now thirty years later, almost at retirement age,
he is still pleased and unrepentant.

QUINTESSENCE

You've only but to crook a finger.
Should you think to raise a brow,
the tides, the winds, all wavering eyes
would not decline to gather you.

No element would dare to linger;
strong winds would huff and shove a vow
aside as Zephyr fumes and sighs,
to banish anguish in Xanadu.

The earth, the air, sluicing water
into plunging furrows plow
for lovers who roar their cries
while pleading for passion's due.

No element in obvious distress
determines by finesse or by caress.

Quotidian

The ranch is empty, but wandering, curious I open
an old barrel almost full of oats. Nothing I know
smells better. Other aromas arrive in close pursuit:
alfalfa, crisp ropes, burning brands and planted hooves,
of sharp-stopping horses jerking down recalcitrant cattle.

More, I remember hitting fungous, scooping
double-plays, judging fly balls, grounders.
We marked the sidelines, learned to keep both feet
in bounds. Punts soared and the discus and shot flew
beyond measured minimums. It was all form, strength,
practice, improvement. The oblong ball
had to leave the passer's hand before the receiver
made his cut. Weights rose and fell next to the tractors,
next to the pen where we kept the calving heifers
that raised us almost once an hour many nights.

The boys are now men, doing what I would
have them do, so why do I sigh when watering
the bougainvillea, the beautiful blood red
bougainvillea along the way to the barn. I see Fall
in the leaves, browning, dropping. The pansies,
such beautiful purple, bow their royal leaves
while I watch football games on television
to discuss along lineless long distance.

I think my father happy now as I breathe deep
and add drops of water to the rich and fallow soil
between the house and barn with no horses
to snort at me, or enjoy old oats.

REASONS TO LIVE IN CISCO

A Response to Q

Because fewer cars parade
than large red ants
churning away in a nest of cracks,
because the sky comes all the way down
to see the droopy eyes
blinking the day away,

because the plumber charges less
than the high school fullback,

because feed-store conversation
drives cattle
to deep fields
where distant cars are not heard
and trains never stop
no matter how hard,
often they sound their horns,

because deer scrape antlers on trees
a little night music with coyote obbligatos
after the sun hides,

and the only lines are in poems.

REFLECTIONS

The moon hurries along
beside my car, trying
to dart-in between
the trees, bounce off
the snow and penetrate
your eyes. My heart races
as I strain to see
myself there too.

Revisited

My maiden aunt Mary came to visit
for a whole month every summer.
She always told the same stories
about how young Jeffery took
her for rides on these same ranch roads
in his 1937 Ford every Sunday
and how he had wanted her
to marry him, but he was killed
in the war. She said nothing
was very nice after that. The traffic
on the highway grew too loud,
and the April roses stopped
smelling so sweet. No romance, she said.

Now I visit her in Dallas once
a month. She says her room
is never warm; the "Villa" reeks
of rubbing alcohol, and the other
residents complain about her blaring TV.
Then she falls asleep while telling me
what has happened this last month
to the various villains, heroes, doctors
and nurses who, between commercials,
come to visit her every day.

SCREEN SAVER

In twenty seconds the computer builds
then disposes of intricate patterns.
(My bald spot grows at about the same speed.)
But beautiful figures which I would keep,
disappear to some unknown terminal
while the world travels toward some black hole,
no known direction, to the gray in my eyebrows,
which hover above me until I dissolve.
I dissolve. My wife, eating ice cream,
stands behind me, smiles, pats my head.

SEEKING SHADE

For thirty years the tree,
already large when we came,
has been some, not complete,
protection from sun,
and even from light rain,
though we have been told
it draws lightening.

I'm told you are an oak,
I take someone's
                            word.

You grow larger as we grow older.
                                        My sons,
I look up to you.
Your leaves reach
                        for the game-room windows,
beckon us,
            but roots
                        worry me.
What do you entail,
                        entangle?
Are you ever satisfied?

Teach us your solid ways;
do not leave us
                    in the dark
with shades.
Come back next year.
We'll be enlightened then.
                            I'm almost sure
I know.

Sirens

Awakening with hard breath
blowing away at the black,
I slip out of the house,
straddle my cycle like a mistress,
crawl between her wheels,
guilty as grease kick her over,
vibrate in the deep rumble
as I roll through the night,
the wind cooling, then burning my thighs,
face. The singing wheels suck me through
the unknown back ways as I roll
the throttle back upon myself
in the dark. I bend into turns,
lean forward to penetrate
between pickups, whose low,
loaded back ends beckon me on.
Swerving in and out,
I believe I can pass them all.

Later, I slide into bed
beside my wife, curl
into position around her like a comma,
wrap myself to her like a mast.

SUDDEN LIGHT

Awakening to light I notice your continued
steady breathing, look out the window,
study the many-colored flitting fluttering thing,
ascending from a cup in an upward helix
as if winding toward higher sweeter
more perfect centers. Teaching others,
escaping to the best places before it forgets.

Where was it in the dark? Did it listen
for regular sounds or was it aroma
dictating safety? Now purposeful moves
put its entirety in proper places.
Under well-mowed grass well-waged wars
rage during the dark in tender light
of early morning. Information by touch,
half the warriors go underground, work
for civilization, order, for continued order.

Flowers have put down roots, hold,
but some turn to light, beginning a DNA
struggle for the chlorophyll green.

I twist, roll to you in my struggle,
curling my legs, pressing my chest on you,
quickly remembering where you are.

The Gulliver Family Curse

Colleagues stop me from pursuing dithyrambs,
truth, beauty, all I need to know. I would converse
with Fussell about etymologies, amphibrachs,
but these yahoos tell me of their daughters' nay-saying husbands,
the sons' unreasonable little bosses. The world picks on their sprung offs
just so they can tell me. I mind. I cannot open
my little end of the conversation as they confess.

Not fair, I bellow, as I leap on my tight wire
lift my head, walk quickly to my office, keep my balance
slam the door. I need the time.
How can I say, take the time to say, my sons
are all doctors, all happy, well-adjusted, handsome,
money-making, loving husbands of beautiful, sweet, intelligent wives,
and perfect fathers, especially when they were such well-known,
famous, to tell the truth, high school, college athletes
they had children named for them.

Because they are loving, sensitive,
thoughtful, kind, solicitous even, I can say nothing.
If I mention their names, I am bragging. How can I confide,
return confidences? I am bereft of decent methods to extinguish
hot air. Not fair, I scream at the laughing gods.

I might say I am inadequate in their presence.
Is this a confidence, or a clever brag?
All seems porous, I've grown so small.
I have to publish. I have to keep up.

I have to write. They will be here
this weekend, shake my hand, kiss me
on the cheek, as they have always done
in public, and private. They will ask me
how goes my poems. How can a man compete?

They may have trouble out-parenting me,
but if they do, they will understand.

THE MAKING OF ONE MORE LAWYER

Watching "Demons" day after MWF day,
far more than six,
he saw them wave,
speak to other gladiators in the hall during class,
scratch themselves, amble out to the bathroom
every time they were bored,
which was once an hour.
They farted, giggled like fourth graders,
brought no notebooks, no textbooks,
but roared indignantly that they had come to class.
Hadn't they been there?
What did he have against athaaleets?

The new M of A climbed on his desk,
shouted, "You are all in the lowest
of three non-transferable, remedial classes
at a non-selective, open-door junior college."

"Remediate, remediate," he commanded.
Spittle slid down his cheek
as they carried him out past the stadium
toward the law school.

The Perfect Mate

You can be anything but Roseanne Barr
or maybe Momma Cass.
I'd like for you to be tall, lean, blonde-
a sort of Princess Grace,
but Audrey Hepburn would be nice.

Don't be impressed by the rich.
Read books, not best sellers.
Understand *The Bridges of Madison County,*
The English Patient are baaad.

No jewels, no perfume, especially no earrings,
no fingernail polish. Be bored by sports.
Love country, classical music.
A glass of wine at the end of some good days is nice.
Walk two miles a day. Be afraid I might die.
Let me calm you. Notice no insults.
Feel sorry for those who hurt,
especially those who hurt you. Love our children
beyond measure. Never watch Jerry Springer.

If you have these ways or don't have them,
understand
you cannot get away from me.
Divorce me,
and I will move in next door to you.
I don't care
if you get to be fat as Roseanne,
don't act like her. I know you
won't. I'll never become John Goodman.
I promise. I can't be Cary Grant,
I'm more like Groucho,
but I'll be a sweet Groucho for you.

THE PRICE OF PERFECTION

My father couldn't make much money
like some guys' fathers, but he could do one thing
perfectly. He could punt a football so high
it came down cold as an empty wallet.

Spirals soared up then the nose turned over.
The ball slid down softly, easy to judge
as how many dollars a bike cost.
On a blustery day, he could float it high
to catch the wind like a dream
Schwynn rolling out of your mind
as the sun shot up.

If he kicked into the wind,
he kept it low like a knuckle ball,
still spiraling, but bumping left, right.
The returner doubted, misjudged,
like a kid not knowing how much cotton candy
he could eat, or the price of things.

He never missed, my father. He looked perfect
to all the guys in my world.
They would watch the ball zip to speck,
then their mouths dropped in an oblong O,
like the sun slowly, slowly setting
on the track circling the pointless field.

Traces

In Memoriam C.H.R. 1900-1966

As you pulled the old horse or mule drawn plow
from its nails on the barn wall, you turned to me,
but looked beyond and forgot your usual flow
about your place in the city's world, the fees
you earned. The life you lifted from the rich
soil again became a part of you.
You laughed at your slow-time pace behind big
wooden hames and crusty traces that knew
the tasks long dropped from new-day thoughts.
We pointed to the lake with the fishing rod
that witched us to the water. We lifted, not bought,
turned-up worms protruding from soft sods
of almost clay with a tenacious hold
on your homesick view of place where I grow old.

WHAT DID IT MEAN?

I'd like to go back to little league games
with the mothers braying: "Hit it for Momma."
They cackled about what they had hatched.
Was it important, their sons in the batter's box,

scratching? I can't remember. The sons have grown
to live with their true wives while the earth spins
out of control in an un-deciphered direction.
Who remembers scores or even big moments?

I think of red snow cones, little brown feet
preparing the earth for strawberry sacrifice.
Tony's behind in the count in a dark slim cage
not meant for batting. Did Tony's attempts to steal

cheers lead him to baseness. Matt Ritchie let
baseballs fall in front of him, while he
stood, legs crossed, chewing on his glove,
dreaming of the day he would run

to the supreme court like Bernard. Did Matt gain
confidence, promise, or did he imagine a field
where he could succeed without nimble feet,
a place to stand without embarrassing his father?

WHAT I THINK I SEE

I see cattle in the next pasture
behind a fence, heads down, wrapping their pink tongues
around long, waving green grass.
They raise their heads, unconcerned, turn
their backs on me, certain there is no other pasture
where grass is sweeter, water cooler.

Time for the school bus
to come crunching in from the farm-to-market,
haul my sons to the rows and rows of desks
in front of the board behind the teacher—a bully
espousing the common cause, hand over her chest
holding nothing in, grasping for dignity.

My wife will leave for four squares of duplicate bridge,
tea, and little finger sandwiches that will leave
her field-hand hungry. She must stop for Perrier
on the way home. The windmill, plunges and plunges.

I must ride every pasture today, count
every calf, admire the rattlesnakes avoiding
the vibrations of non-prey too big to eat.
I look at cactus flowers, guess how much water
they sucked up from the sinking table.
My yellow dog trails behind my horse, happy
to go where I go. He stops, raises his head
to listen to the hollow sounds
riding the wind, tries to see what might be.

I see my father ahead of me, going over a rise,
following three coyotes, looking for the disappearing moon.
He smiles, motions me on, gestures toward the east
where mother always wanted him.
He sticks one finger in the air, waves it
back and forth like the flag man on the back
of the last car of a long train. He smiles
after the school bus, exhausting itself up the hill
toward the sun. I reign-up, decide I will
see my father tomorrow, perhaps, on this trail.

WHEN I HOLD YOU, YOU FIT

Our two histories crossed paths
like merging drops
of water blown about on car windows.

Cool rain on canted surfaces
slips to the earth and flows for ages
to the sea. Clouds come back to be
as they always have been.

I take your cold hand;
you accept my warmth.
We see through dappled windows—
a land with boundaries
and bays that separate
only the surface of islands
joined by narrow bridges.

Our fingers entwine,
slowing the flow of blood.
I feel our pulse and count
slowly steadying beats.

WILL

Grandfather William was lean as a whip.
He wore vested suits,
coat buttoned to the top.
A great gray mustache hid an upper lip I never saw.

He never bent in the saddle,
not at a gallop,
not going through brush.
His hat never blew off.

He was eighty-one
when I rode to his house to see him
at the hitching post
beside a banging kitchen door,
struggling to lift his heavy saddle
to the back of a big bay horse.

His arms were shaking as he held the saddle
pinned between his chest and the bay.

He looked at me with moist eyes,
dropped the saddle in the dust.

He looked at the bay, shifted his blue eyes to my face.
"I never rode a horse cept I saddled it."
He looked at the empty house
where my father was born
"I'd have to stay here, wouldn't I?"

"Yes, Grandpa, you would," I said,
reaching for the saddle,
old and cracked at his feet.

READING HOMETOWN OBITUARIES

She looked like Judy's good witch, Billie Burke,
whose floating wand waved a floating caress.

With not so much a hurried push or ram
as a sliding wiggle, I could squirm
through, after Saturday double feature matinees,
almost to the front of the blinding, mirrored light
where Judy Fey buried her hand right
in the sure and holy depth of all goodness.
With her cap a laurel, a halo in florescent rays,
she lifted almost all young distresses,
scooping high from a bin of hard pure white.

I confirm I remain a vanilla-loving man.
My eyes transfixed, worshipped at her short sleeves,
as she extracted creamy fingers, knuckles.

I feared an empty, wicked spell—a drought
before my flattened nose. She rapidly circled
above her container-demense, a diurnal breeze,
cyclonic even, asking, "Single dip or double?"
In heat before conditioned air, no doubt
two scoops could drip to elbow trouble,
but who worth a dime could say, "Single, please."

Even though your enchantments could turn to mess,
I pray you may remain in the bewitching goodness,
loving, lovely Judy Mary Fey Lauck,
whose sweet caress could shame the actress Billie Burke.

You Can't Depend on Me

I see pictures of us forty years younger,
my student ID card, your picture in the yearbook,
don't understand why you took
my name. You look sensible, but
more beautiful than reason.

Not the bread winner,
embarrassed as the toe
in the carpet I drug
behind you, you,
turned to me
in front of the clerk,
asked what we could afford,
what you could have.

You can have anything
you want, anything I can possibly get for you,
though you continue to ask.

FAMILY VACATION IN THE MOUNTAINS

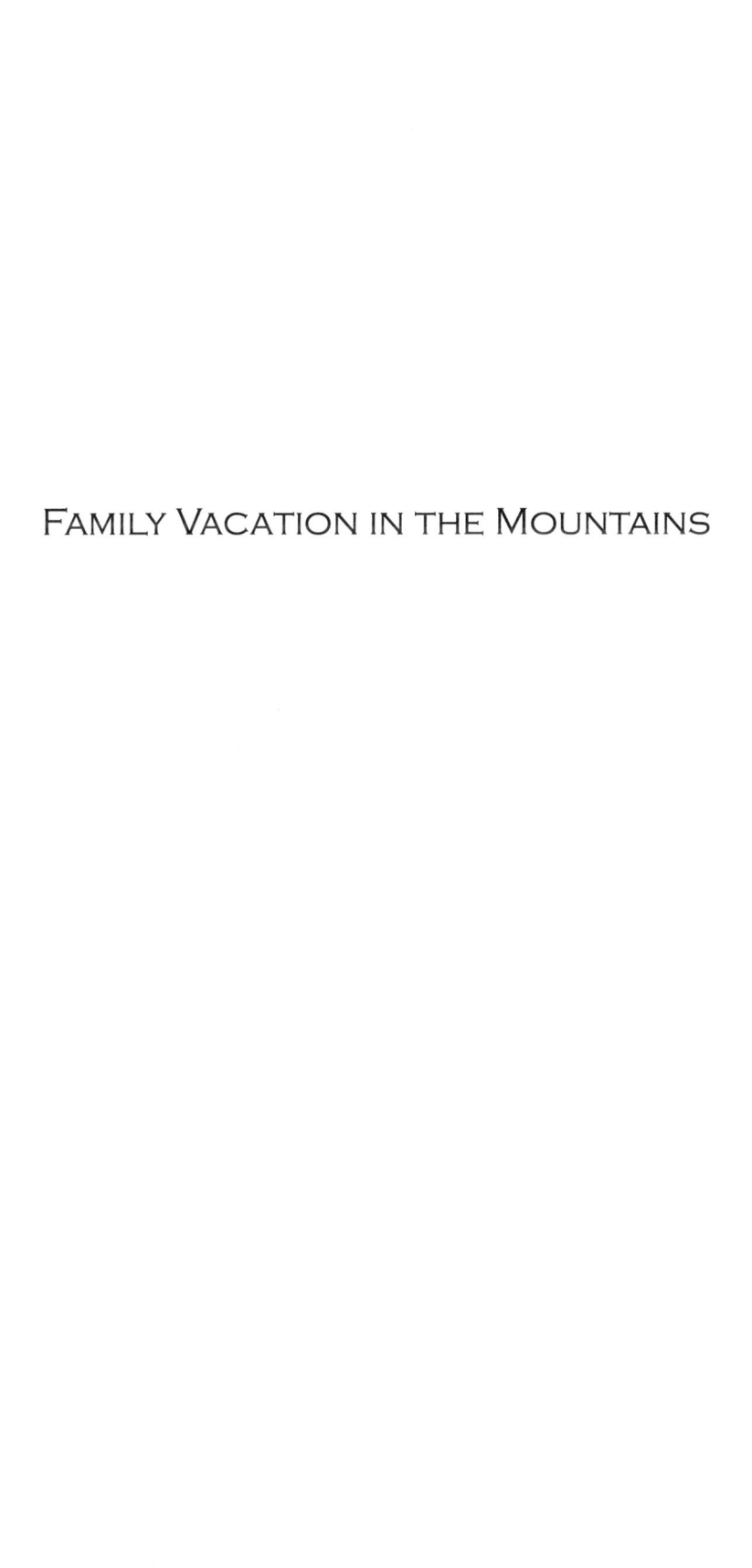

AT THE "O" CLUB IN OKINAWA

For Our Beloved Corps

An old colonel, maybe thirty-six or so,
lean, brown, and hard as Aunt Grace's
butter churn talked loudly about
the how of the war,
never mentioned the why.
Captains or under talked about women,
football, cars.

The colonel, pointed, exclaimed left hand waving,
weighed down by his BFR from the academy.
A major in '65—battalion logistics—
he held a regiment in '69.
He was a gimme for a star.

The field grade officers knew from Quantico
eight chances out of ten they'd take a hit in a year,
retire a purple-hearted major, with luck.
No new odds in a second tour.

The colonel had no wife, nothing
but a retired M/Sgt. father in California,
his ring, and an expensive whore
with enough rouge to camouflage contempt
for stories killing time.

A letter from recently retired,
promoted in-hospital, First Lieutenant
Ronald P. Pajardo indicated he entered
civilian ranks with twenty-one months
in the Corps, three months in-country,
and an empty sleeve pinned to his coat
like a note from his mother.
His wife was happy to hold onto
the full sleeve, buoyed
by 100% disability pay.

Bobby Davis' Fate

Bobby Davis was a dope who failed an important unit of history
almost taught by Coach Lehmberg
to football players. Coach had earlobes
that hung almost to his shoulders. When he listened,
he slanted his head left to see the vision
coming at him. When he spoke, he snapped his head toward you,
slinging earlobes in a wide arc.
You heard his eyes click, ducked his slanted vision.

Howard Perdue lost no time convincing Coach
to see Bobby taking us to unseen, unfelt heights
of football glory. He was almost right. Bobby passed,
ran hard, but Breckenridge beat us like truant children.
Bobby, armed with a high school diploma, qualified
to cradle an M-16 to the point
where he ducked when he heard a click, but misplaced his foot.

Hobbled, Bobby crutched his way home with his head down,
looked left, right for a sitting-down job.
He was snapped-up like a booby trap
by a fellow veteran who taught Bobby to work a crane at a place
where he could raise a high-grade machine several hundred feet
above the civilized buildings squatting on the surface
of an exploding city. Bobby never talked about the history
of his unit in Nam, ducked his head into chemically induced
punji stick after stick that blew his frontal lobes.

A 45 slug spread his spirit over a slanted spire he raised
to salute mankind's fate.

CHRISTMAS IN SEATTLE ON THE EVE
OF WAR

The woman walks into the strong wind
from the west. Her dress wraps around her,
slows her movement. The man coming at her
slows his pace, notes the fullness of desire,
follows her in his mind until even there she closes
the door. He sighs silently for packages
he may never open, gifts never given.

COSMIC

After five years a Marine, three years
between visits, he appears to his family:
visitation by a stranger in a well-lighted room.
Back slaps, like shocking thunder,
boom in his ears while black eyes
in white faces; eyes, eyes he can see himself in,
try to take him in.
He slips back to dark nights
where brothers from a larger family
looked up at white stars, too many
to count, at slivers of light
flickering off never fully known.

DISCREET

Staff Sergeant Ronald L. Stearns saved
me. On patrol we came upon a snake
entangled about a tree. Its coffin black
deep eyes reflecting, taking us in. Its tongue

flicking, its scales more ancient than war,
its open, yellowed mouth caverned. Stearns
grabbed me, motioned me to step around
the old serpent. Twelve of us stepped far

away from an ominous presence, laughed,
or protested Judas-like, later. We made
our rendezvous with the retrieval copter,
returned to base. Late afternoon, the Staff

and I walked the slimy streets of Saigon
when one of the Sallys captured me,
her eyes entrancing, massaging. I looked
into her pink mouth as she held on,

telling me what she could do for a price. Her hair
was black, complexion peach. I haggled hard
until I felt the staff prod, comfort me,
asking: "When will you ever learn, sir?"

Family Vacation in the Mountains

On some unpredictable occasions when the
wrong brain is in charge, I see mountain ridges
from my car, think in clicks*, look for coordinates
on an overlay in my wife's lap as chopper

blades scorn flattened land. Brake lights bring me
back on a path Stearns can't find. A hot landing
zone burned him beyond reorganization
in a mud-pie paddy. His head in helmet,

foot in boot, he was protected from an open
casket warm endorsement from his country.
We had been cracking jokes like nuts buried in
slimy warm water, crouching from rockets

he may have seen the red glare of. I lifted
Bill Graves like prayer to corpsmen in the door,
watched him burst in on eternity's edge, consecrate
the ground he rained on. I've waded endlessly

in doctor's offices, afraid of vile blood,
remembered Pajardo with no arm. His blood
filled the hole he sweated over all day,
digging for time away from eternity.

His white bones in a geyser of red, ruins re-visions
of old faithful land my wife finds beautiful.

*Clicks is a measurement of distance to help the aim. Rifles and
mortars have different meanings for the distances.*

FRIENDLY FIRE

Daring to churn through Uncle Sammy's puff-white, blue sky
a check mark of four steel-gray, iron-winged Skyhawks
slipped in to burst an orange bubble
slightly above the heads
of fourteen pieces
of two men
placed in
one bag.

The wind raises the surface then rolls on toward the mountains,
stretches the desert, deposits grains that wait
to grow with ever greater numbers.
What was high stays high,
churning what was living
to the indiscriminate
moment.

Honor

My father was the point of the triangle
as I was flanked by uncles. Mother was distant,
sobbing slightly, out of sight behind the barn.
Honor was father's word, and I took
my usual bracing stance when he used it.
He looked into my eyes. Uncles were quiet
as ex-marines on parade. He put too much money
into my hand: "Go to your war, if you must,
but come home with your shield or without it."

The sun and moon have circled and hidden
each other many times since that day.
I have seen my rings of friends broken
in flames, had my luck, but I have never
been richer than that glaring moment
when mother's eyes were red as cinders.

I TOLD HIM

(The End of the Affair)

During delivery on Angel wings from Vietnam,
a French Captain, an observer, asked me
if I wanted to read *Paris Match.*
He frowned when I pretended to read every word
until fate made me ask him about the details of a story
about an American football player,
signing for beaucoup more money than twenty generals.
Americans had no real sense of value *PM* said.
The captain smiled in agreement with *PM.*
"*Je pense que ils ont raison,*" I said.

Unable to command the French, I told the captain
in English that the RB had cloven hooves.
A smile broad as his arrogance,
indicated his pleasure in the weakness
of the American Lieutenant's French.
But the Captain had missed something diabolical.

Mutual commiseration about the war ended
when I hissed in unmistaken English:
"Dien Bien Phooey
as a Khe Sahn point."

IN A DRUG STORE IN L.A. IN 2012

Seeking sleeping pills at 1 AM,
wearing a Marine Corps Ball Cap
an old fart, my age, asked me
if I ever killed anyone. "Yes," I told him.
He said, "Why?" "Because I was there,
I told him." He disapproved. I hadn't
had this conversation in years. I was nineteen
when I joined the Corps. Ten years later,
commanding a Company out of An Loc
on a sweep, we began to take hits.
My kids, my men, were falling. I hear them yet.
We suppressed the fire. I called in artillery.
Soon there was no village. I did not send a patrol
to see (assess) the damage, which was hard
to explain. I did not want to know
about fragments. "Good arty*," a young,
battle weary sergeant told me. Minutes later
we loaded six of us, four moaning,
on helicopters and continued our stroll.

* "Arty" is a slang word for artillery. Sergeants are fond of young
lieutenants who do not need several rounds fired to get on target.

THAT LOOK

The doctor came out of swinging doors, looking
like my mother coming out of the kitchen,
but not eager. She pulled off her cap,
no longer needing to worry about falling hair.

She looked at my insignia, determined
I was the Marine she saw before.
Her eyes searched her shoes; she watched her step,
tired enough to fall. Her eyes caught
mine then dropped again, finally searched
my eyes when she was close enough
to breathe with me. Her eyes clouded
as she told me what I already knew.

She looked toward the ceiling
like a saint remembering something,
looking for Angels like Titian's *Europa.*
She was Botticelli's *Venus*, failing
to find complete cover with hands
that failed her hopes.

I remember her expressions, changing
minute by minute. Almost every day,
especially when someone, often me, looks for God,
I see her sad eyes.

TOYS

A toy soldier in the yard
by the big oak, formerly third base,

is at high port, striding, not ready to kill,
a pellet wound in his raised right thigh.

His buddies are gone under grass, leaves, mortar
chips, in an uncivilized, well-controlled lawn.

Maneuvered on the brick—a fortress
squaring the tree—he is a lookout, on point.

Comrades will recover, rally round him
on second tours, and become targets
for indigenous, insurgent birds,
melting sun, brittle cold, and prey for forces
neither seen nor understood.

He does his duty,
what he was made for.

The Great Doak Walker

A FICTION

My words fall short, never make the name
exactly right, never fit a page, lie in the dirt,
try to squirm away, embarrassed.
I follow them down with slitted eyes,

feeling their vibrations, their clanging symbols.
Father called, worried about my ability,
tells me I'm dim, threatens to enlighten me.
Out of his interest, his garden, I am unsure

how I can make him happy. Without you,
Daddy, I'm lost. If you will listen to reason,
my thoughts will reach toward a coherent heaven,
pick themselves up, gather on the page,

push through rows, lines, on the eve,
the beginning of naming something big.
Help me. I'll look up to you if you do.
Wouldn't you enjoy that?

Can These Flowers Live?

Maiden Aunt Mary, always Maiden Aunt
Mary, hair short as the heels
on her black shoes, read the bible
every hour she wasn't sewing or gardening
or dressing to go to town for church.
She read to prove she had missed
nothing. Satisfied by nothing
but the prophets and hell's fire,
she made no bones about her perennials
and planted way up there in the middle
of the north pasture, her purple violets
and other flowers no one here has names
for now. They are there, still defying
cash crops, fleshing out each year
and blessing, always blessing,
Momma's grave and Poppa's.
Cars stop and men take off their hats,
then mop their brows while women
take pictures, preserving forever
the acres of purple flowers
in the middle of cotton,
replanted year after year.

A TOUR

A bus will remain locked in place, diesel
running, pouring poison heavenward, while I lie dying
of some slowly disabling disease,
coughing into my initial-embroidered handkerchief.

I will hear mourners on the street, moaning,
singing hymns. My house will become a shrine
like Cockermouth or Nether Stowey.
People will visit where I was cinched

by the Bible Belt, underrated, under-understood.
"Tsk, tsk," (somebody must say) or "Oh Lordy,"
he lived all his life with indifference from boors'
blissful ignorance. Unpaid, un-rescued

he was unrecognized until too late.
People will look on walls for hieroglyphs,
under boards, where treasure may lie,
a disintegrating, forgiving diary, perhaps.

The indigenous folk will deny they knew
my pain. Heads will bow, brochures fold,
wrinkle. The pilgrims will cluck, tsk again,
leave no wiser but determined to tell where they

have been, what pulse they felt. They will be
purified. I will have been subdued by infinite laws
to the useful and the good. My spirit understands,
forgives the infinite folk to God's thunderous applause.

THE GREAT DOAK WALKER

At a point slightly northeast of the goal,
slightly outside the ivy-fed stadium, a circle
where brick walks converge from three paths,
escorted by long wide rows of red bougainvillea,
deep purple pansies, scarlet and blue, the sun,
the sea, created to show the way to the nave,
this Parthenon, this statue of the great Doak Walker,
poet of placement. He leans right, cleats holding,
left knee bent to place his foot on hallowed ground
where would-be tacklers hazard predictions
of its next coming. No one but him can detect
soft breezes sweeping the chalice he caresses.
Helmeted warriors worship, bow, pay homage
to the spondaic substitutions of his rhythmic feet,
as the wind from Olympus whispers his every step.

Football in Texas

God gave us Bach, Beethoven, Mother Teresa,
Dr. Schweitzer, and Doak Walker.

No one can do what Bach did every day.
Believe, evidence exists. It is hard to see
when war brings out the best in us. We who are greedy,
sacrifice in war. Shaking afraid of moles turning dark
in peace, we brave blistering death over and again in war.

Beauty is the miracle. Ice-skating is beautiful.
Bougainvillea is natural beauty, and maybe Halle Berry
and Jennifer Anniston for instance,
as well as the voice of Elvis.

In Texas we are said to worship football.
Look to Doak Walker. See   .
his beauty as he performed miracles on Fridays,
Saturdays, Sundays for fourteen years.
Get the film, watch one miracle for example:
With the miracle of recorded events, seek him
for yourself. You can decide what a miracle is,
but search is required.

In a game in college, against Rice,
Doak was back to punt and the ball went sailing
far over his head. He turned to run after the ball
when it jumped into his arms, by chance, maybe.
He was running full-blast parallel with the goal
about fifty yards away, punted the ball straight to his left—
forty-six yards, out of bounds. No one can do that.
Get the film.

All, no exceptions, of Doak's teammates in high school,
college, and pros agree he made them better,
and they expected him to pull them out of the fire.
He almost always did. When he didn't, every witness knew
the forces of this world, good and bad, were formidable.
Matthew and Luke disagree, but not D's teammates.

FORECAST

(Mark 4:26-29)

The sky is full threat; the wind billows
black clouds from the mountains.
The calving heifers twitch tails
in the stable, ignored by horses
and cats who live by milk, mice.
My son and I scan the valley for our collie,
but, pursuing some heavenly scent
he is far from the electricity that runs off,
guilty. By fire and flashlight, I read
of the prodigal. At the door during lightning
strikes we hear our dog, whimpering.
My son pulls the wet, smelly beast in, hugs
him to a place by the fire, covers dirty
matted hair with a good towel as I turn
to the parable of the seed sown.

I EXPECT

I expect Jesus to come back as first trombone,
poo pooing the Mikado. He will be blaring
a deep, rumbling harmony for Al Hirt or Tommy Loy.
Certainly he won't be fluting around like Artie Shaw's
or Pee Wee's clarinet sticks, above the melody. I bet
He lets Woody Allen sit in occasionally on a few sets.
Jesus could plunk bass fiddle, I suppose, but never plinking
a piano from chord to chord, playing by ear—never.
No, He will get his aggregation together, playing
The Tin Roof Blues, with many drummers, letting the Dukes
of Dixieland blow in for a set or two. Or maybe
the Asunto brothers can render *St. James Infirmary*.
Then we will all know what time it is in
and get together for real unwritten harmony.
And nobody will play *When The Saints Come Marching In.*
Well, maybe the Blues Brothers with Aretha could.

TO MAKE GOD

We all know the story of three wishes.
A favorite is the story of three countrymen
of slightly different colors who share an island.

When the giver of wishes offers one wish
to representatives of each group, the first, a swarthy type,
asks for the other two types to be removed from the island.

The second man, a black man, wishes the swarthy
and the whites taken way. The Englishman says,
"Could I have a pink gin, please."

The point of this story, as most understand,
is that mankind of all types has no notion
what to do with wishes.

No one wish ever comes true but for a moment, and
"The difference betwixt benefit and injury"
lies beyond the island.

To make God stop laughing,
stop telling him wishes, have a pink gin.

Journeys

A blind man with his stick believes in magic
wands, his palm callused as the sky.

Not a person wandering, window shopping,
looking for his image, but like a comet
he deliberately sweeps his path,
tapping like a lover on a window,
resigned as a train entering a hollow station.

He travels alone, feeling for blessings
until his stick strikes an obstacle,
and like an army under siege
he is unable to advance.

Wounded, he retreats into the safety
of a woman who
gives him of what is beyond.

JUST CRUISING

"Before God and with God we live without God."
Dietrich Bonhoeffer, qtd in A New Christianity for a New
World.*—John Shelby Spong

Cruisers like to dance and gamble. Wives
enjoy cruising too. They know
after the exercise of the dance to attend
to spinning wheels.

Waltzing across the Atlantic in three-quarter time,
sleep comes like it must have,
rocking in the special fluid
of mothers, but the fish looking up to us
feel relieved when we pass on.
They pray to us to dance over them
one more time. It is only a little more time.

They feel the vibrations of feet. They see
spinning screws, broken ships lying about, decaying.
They are as uncertain of us as we are
of the spinning wheel.

My poor fishy kin, I weave no nets,
throw no hooks, but offer you no help.
It has always been so. Bonhoeffer said so,
and he had reason.

*Probably quoted from The Cost Of Discipleship by Bonhoffer

NOTHING COMES EASY

but everything entertains me. I don't want
the sun to go down or come up,
it does all the time—a certain revolution.

Around, around like a baseball game,
lop-sided, asymmetrical, nine against one,
one against no time limit, will it never end?

I'd love for games to go on forever,
but when the time comes for travel,
I allow all games to end. You have to

replay them, if you can. You have to replay
them. I love to see the illumined
little sphere coming closer, going away

from me by my force. I am
one who can't stop what he started.
I'm obliged to circular reasoning.
That ball has to move according to rules.

ONLY TWICE

What about seven times seven or seventy

I wanted to be Paul Newman
twice. Do you remember Verdict?
He was a loner, a failure, a lost attorney
who drank too much, but his clothes
always looked nice, and his hair
was always cut perfectly. He was neat.

He won his case in spite of the world
that is always against non-conformists,
and he was alone as if he were on the Pequod
or maybe the man against the sky, mumbling
something about standing among them,
but not being of them.

Paul finally got help from Charlotte Rampling.
Like him she was alone, down and almost out,
but she was a spy, a traitor. He punched her,
knocked her down in the court house,
though he had won his case.

He defeated the forces of evil,
and he was again alone,
the man never satisfied. He sat in his office
with the phone ringing. Charlotte wanted something
of him, but he had nothing to give.

I would have said to her: "Come on over
none of us can resist all temptation.
Let's have a drink, and I will put something on your eye
and we can take our specks out."

The second time I wanted to be him
he was "involved" in a libel case absent of malice
with a reporter who wanted everyone to love her.
Remember Sally's acceptance speech: "You like me,
you really like me." Poor thing,
but she had a fine figure, really nice.

Paul taught her a few things, and like Henry James' Newman,
he sailed away not having to worry about money.
He was headed up the east coast by himself
in his own boat. She would have been
fine company, and as she watched him motor, later sail
off, we knew what he knew. She wanted to go.

If he had asked her, I would have felt better
like watching a movie hero take a drink
when I'm thirsty. She would have filled his cup,
but no, our heroes move on, though usually west.

THE BLESSING

It was a day to hunt
not to tend to other chores.
My tri-colored collie, though
no good as a hunting dog

always enjoyed the romp.
Out of the pick-up she went
her way. She'll find me later,
I thought. I walked straight

as virtue north with my almost
useless 410 crooked under
my arm. The deep meadow grass
waved me along in the southerly

breeze. Thinking to check along
the east fence, I turned left
for 100 yards. Finding no rabbits
hiding in holes, I followed my path

back to the original rut in the middle
of the meadow. On briefly north
then seeing a way to cross
the creek, I came back and trekked

west through the creek, then up
the hill to sit and watch the sun
lower itself. My collie came
running far below me following

my scent. She was perfect north—
east then west to the pure
water where she lost me.
She followed the same route

over and over, believing
she could find me. I waved
my crooked, breached scepter,
but she could not find me.

I sat content to watch her
invoke blessing after blessing.

THREE SHADES OF GREEN

In neat space with clear borders,
the page tells of the loss of Beverly,
Kay, and Carolyn yesterday or early last night.
Beverly (66) attended expensive schools
as did her granddaughter Kay (21).
Beverly made good grades, did everything right,
married right, belonged. Kay, the recent graduate,
was coming out, but she failed
to straighten one last curve in her new Lexus.

Carolyn (29) attended the local junior college
until she fell, sick with cancer. She left a daughter
of the house with a husband, a plumber
not of the same name as the daughter.

Perhaps the Greens crossed the river,
smiled at the Ferryman together.
Or maybe climbed a gangplank, linking arms,
if shades have anything like arms to link.
Not two by two this time.

It all seems so neat, their lying there, side by side by side
in black and white. Do they inhabit a stateroom, navigating
a flood, a tide so large that ferrymen, arkmen starting over,
must hurry. Do the pilots, you think, ever tire,
stay on the other side? And if they do, do you suppose
they stop occasionally to speak clear, tidy paragraphs
with a few former passengers? Which ones?

Saddle Up

A FAREWELL PARTY

For Johnny

I rode by your house today
the first time since.
The gate was open and a bull
calf was on the porch.
Something sucked the tail
of your checkered curtain
out of a broken window.
It waved me away, waved goodbye.
I turned to leave, but then I
remembered the way you would
begin to hum some tuneless song,
pull your hat far down
on your head and how your eyes
lit up when you began to build
your loop. I came back,
eased the sorrel you liked
through the gate, and chased
the motley-faced intruder
into the already sagging
fence, then roped and dragged
the arrogant black beast back
where he belonged. I smiled
thinking of your approval
then laughed and laughed
until my vision blurred.
I turned the sorrel loose
to feed on cactus flowers
and tried to watch
as the sun slid off somewhere.

What Comes of Home Burial

I must ride by sometimes.
I try not to look at the land.
It's the sky that blankets all.
A little land that one becomes
is too small. I imagine mother, father
down there. I hear them calling me
to come to them. Their voices louder,
stronger than the day father urged me
to step from the high board
at the club pool.

From even a slight distance above,
the tops of tombs
must seem like cornices of windows
seen from the street. The fence around Momma,
Poppa, Aunt Mary, what for?
The dead come closer each trip to the south pasture.
I beg their blurred faces: let me pass.

The ways of dying are numerous as the ways of living.
I fear them all.
Poppa, the day of your death
was dark but with pinholes of light
light streamers of bright ribbons
to show the way.

Send some sign, a sacrament, a creed,
a myth, a doctrine, some kind message for your inheritor,
passing by your fence, looking above your window,
who has no understanding.

ALL OVER AGAIN

A hame-headed, big bay horse splashed with white
on his chest and face belonged to my youngest boy.
Almost a year it took to break and train

the mule-headed bang tail. Nearly impossible
to catch, he planted back hooves, lifted front
ones, and whirled as fast as any ancestor

dodging predators in trees. My son, about twelve,
would race home from school to ask if his horse
was ready, but blaze face was sly. He'd go a month

just fine, then when he thought I focused only
on calves through loops, he'd blow like Sunday
sirens. My wife saw the tops of fence posts under his belly

from the kitchen. I should have sold him
years ago. Old now, he meets me at the gate
impatient for a feed-bucket tribute. He prances, pawing,
snorting bravado, daring me to put that boy on his back again.

April Roses

Every summer but one when I was in high school
Mr. Burney's granddaughter, Evelyn,
with her mother, came to visit for a month.

She was always too late for the April roses
mother's man was so good with. I wished for her,
and the roses to come at the same time.

I would see Evelyn at the Episcopal Church
and understand that I would have to try to negotiate
a new horse a half-mile or so down the dusty road

to the Burney place. Young horses and roads with occasional
cars often fail to blend, but to see her in the black
or white shorts jutting down to the tops of bronze thighs

was thrill enough to trust some young sorrel horses,
with blaze faces that my father always preferred,
and I slipped out of the gate, chanced my way,

tied my horse by the kitchen door and Evelyn would come out,
move her almost white hair back from her face to kiss
me on the cheek before her grandmother got to the door.

I had seen enough movies to know to bring flowers,
yellow roses that grew close to our front gate,
but never the April red ones that I wanted for Evelyn.

Not long after my arrival, Mr. Burney's phone would ring
and he would laugh and tell father that the sorrel
was a good-looking horse, and that I would be home "directly,"

but I would stay longer just to show I was grown enough
to have some independence. Evelyn and I went to movies
downtown at the Rialto or to the drive-in on the Brownwood road.

She wore shorts to the drive-in and tight skirts to the Rialto.
Each had its advantage. Ninth grade summer I put my hand on her
breast, and she laughed. I think she laughed because I

didn't move my hand, just left it there, and she laughed.
Tenth grade summer, I put my hand under her black shorts.
Eleventh grade summer Evelyn arrived late because she and mother

had taken an attenuated grand tour. She came back breathless
to tell me of Florence where men pinched her.
She laughed again until her family went to Brownwood

to see *Ben Hur.* Her bra and shorts came off somehow,
and I vowed to marry her. I almost always made her
laugh. Senior summer she wrote to tell me that she had gone

to Dallas to start summer school at SMU. I went to SMU
that fall, and she was pinned to a football player.
She married him that next summer and soon had a baby boy.

She is a Methodist now. I see her with sons some summers,
too late for red roses, visiting her grandmother. Her dark hair
is short. She smiles, holds up the yellow rose I send.
The drive-in closed, though I see *Ben Hur* on TV occasionally.

Draggin Calves

Before the red sun
stares the white moon into hiding,
you saddle-up
and trot slowly out to gather the herd
with just a touch
of morning moisture on your face.
You find them and start back
half-hoping one or two mammas
with babies beside make a break.

If they do, you can cowboy.
Spur your horse and run hard
round mesquite, through brush
and over ditches.
Rein him up and drive his back
legs so far in the dirt
his ass scrapes the ground.

Once you have the calves penned,
you rope and drag
them to the fire.

The cowboys on the ground
castrate, de-horn, notch the ears
and brand.

The mommas bellow
while one at a time
(maybe remembering)
they come to the hissing red glow
to watch
white-eyed.

CELEBRATION AFTER SCRIBBLING
SEEMS SILLY

I never know what to do after having written.
I tire of TV, news, and movies.
Most often, I walk to the barn and admire the horses.
I feed them oats to watch them eat. They can't
napkin their lips and that removes a great deal
of tiring judgment. They can masturbate,
and I admire that. Without thumbs it is a remarkable accomplishment,
and they are careless masturbaters, another fine quality
without puritan judgments. Well trained, they work hard,
enjoy the work I have for them. They don't demand
I talk to them, but they don't mind when I do.
Even with such fine long necks, they don't look back
as much as I do. They look up though.
Predators may be above them, they know. Their defense
is a quick rider dumping jump to the side.

They never worry about productivity;
they take their oats and grass and hay as they find them.
They never hide their heads in maps, pose for pictures,
or worry about aging. They take their age as it finds them.
Most important, the present only toucheth them;
not looking backward, they never plan.
Posterity, the problem for all writers, produces no concern.
If a big cat jumped on their necks from trees,
boulders or anything above them, they would look up
no more than ever. Never having seen a tyger,
they know the possibility exists.

One could do worse than worry only about big birches
bending toward earth, holding big boogy cats.

EVIDENCE

When all is frozen, sounds stop.
No whir from the windmill. Leaves
can't rustle. Squirrels hide in holes.
Birds turn tail to the wind and swell.
On these nature-quiet days we violate
the scheme, make noise with foot and wheel
to feed the cattle, chop the ice. Everywhere
we go our dirty tracks and crunching
sounds show and shout through crystal air.

First Light

Saddling my horse in the early morning
dark, I try to remember how many high-headed
colts have become heavy, resigned old horses
under my saddles. How many times have I
stood at the gate feeling for the latch
fearing a snake might be near? Have I
known where dangers lay? Trotting
out further in the black, I wonder
if my father had such thoughts
on this road. Will my sons
wait for the amber glow of morning
on this way?

When I see the outline of cow
and calf in the beginning
light, I put aside these thoughts
one more time.

FREE OF THE FLESH

A cowboy's bones
are always trying to escape. You can feel
them when you pull your horse
to a quick stop and sit
down hard in the saddle.
You can see their marks in your jeans;
the bones are not content
to come through the flesh
but must wear two shiny spots
in the seat of Levi's best.

The summer the college boy came
to work for us he roped
a sour calf that had been roped
twice too often. When the cowboy
pitched his slack, the calf felt
the noose around his neck and turned
back to the horse like a prodigal
trying to escape the wrenching jerk.
The rope poised in the air,
neatly danced to figure eight
and dropped quickly around
the slack-pitching hand
still in the air as if to ask
a question. The horse stopped hard;
the calf ran hard, and the bones
stood out white as maggots
in a fountain of blood.

The doctor placed pins
in the bones, pulled
skin around them again
then whispered
to the bones,
"Be patient, be patient."

Looking Deep

Occasionally when trotting out
to far away work across the creek
Johnny and I see fish. They are different
sizes and shapes, but like the old men
and ladies at church they all look
much the same. One comes up
to stare then returns to his group
bubbling about something deep.
Another breaks away, leaves protection
of his kind and comes to register
astonishment. With only a quick look
through the sometimes clear water
he returns to a safe dark place
to nod in agreement with friends
about things above them all.
Johnny, my friend, sits on his roan
and says it is a seasonal thing
the fish are going somewhere.
He suspects they don't know where.
His insights are good enough for me.
The world is full of secrets.

Grandsons of the Pioneers

Looking for Gene and Roy

The Saturday afternoon matinees:
guns flashing under white hats and black, red
and white popcorn shell casings littering
the only safe aisles out of town. Roy, Gene,

good as they were, and no doubt real cowboys,
were not like the bouncing asses you see today
galloping fro and to the camera. Roy would drop
his guitar, leap in the saddle, duck bullets,

chase cars, head them off after having found
a short cut known only to horsemen. But wherever
Roy, Gene lived, cars, horses were pals.
Froggy always urged his car along,

helping the chase. Bad guys honked from
the road, the car riders, safe in faux naugahyde,
laughed to see the tops of fence posts under
my horse's belly, then sped away with my
trail blocked by the cursed barbed wire.

MORNING RITUALS

I saddle my horse in darkness and ride north
to the lake, looking for new calves. I must know
no golden hereford has slipped into greener
fields. She opens the french doors to the patio
and sees the green, blue water of the pool.
Her eyes reflect the liquid as she sees a touch
of morning moisture on a red-wood table
holding amber juice and dark toast.
Her golden, layered hair ripples gently
in the wind like clouds flowing opposite
directions at different heights. Brown leaves
in the pool blow back and forth,
growing larger, smaller, floating
beneath rising mist. My big bay horse,
impatient, stabs the lake edge with his hoof,
shakes his body to say that we have looked
enough at murky reflections. She opens
yesterday's paper, uninterested in daily things.
A big bronze cat catches her eye
as it climbs the fence, eager for the barn.
I scan the north mountains
that roll in thunder. She steps back
in the house to wake our sons
for school. I turn south,
eager to learn her flesh again.

ON CALF ROPING

The first thing to do
after your filly is warm
is check your equipment.
Tighten your cinch.
When the calf darts right then left
and all your weight shifts,
things better hold.
Tighten the flank strap.
She could get hurt
in the withers.
Don't forget the skid pads.
A horse burned,
skidding
won't stop for you again.
Tighten your rope hard
to the horn that sticks up
in front of you.
Build your loop;
put the piggin string in your mouth.
get her in the roping box easy,
back her till she touches.
Now wait.
The calf must look forward.
Your horse must relax.
The chute opens;
you're THRUST in the arena.
This is the excitement,
the brief moment
you can almost remember.
The calf might run hard
for the back end
or maybe run dirty
darting left right.
Stay close.
EXPLODE
your loop.
Run down the rope,
tie.

You walk back to your horse
exhausted,
satisfied.

ON ROPING, LUSTING,
AND BLOOD PRESSURE

In front of me, all white, acting efficiently
she takes my arm, extends it along her hip bone.
Palm up, pumped up and wrapped up sufficiently
I see her legs and indented zone.

Sighing, I leave to get my horse and rope.
The clustered calves explode from the chute.
After them, I throw my loop and hope.
A miss. My abilities in hot pursuit

are declining. I tie an imagined calf. Arms
in the air I signal victory over leisure.
The horse, power between my legs, has charms
and what the hell, he relieves the pressure.

THE MIDDLE

About halfway to the pens
across the creek
I tell Johnny
that after four days
working cattle
my hands are blistered
my back sore
and if I flank
one more calf
that throws its head
back into my knee
I'll be too stove up
to mount my green-broke filly
for the ride back to the barn.

He listens to the distant windmill whir
spits brown tobacco juice
on the green cactus
we can never be rid of
and says, "You're at the cowboy
in between age—to old to outwork
and out rope the kids
but too young
to enter
the oldtimer ropings."

I refuse to smile
and hide my dreams
like the raw flesh
under my gloves.

WARNINGS

I heard the odd little bird
whose name you probably
know go into his charade.

He dips low, flies a side-slip
as if he's hurt. Sometimes
he runs a burlesque, a clipped-

wing bird screaming someone
or thing away from his nest—
his show amusing the sun.

I wondered who was watching
the show often reserved for me.
I stumbled back to the spring

behind a ridge guarded by oak
and brush. A trucker who scaled
my fence walked past the joke

with an empty jug. He needed
something from nature and more,
but birdie accepted no deed

that might prove danger to his breed.
The bird and I watched his chore,
hidden and suspicious of man's need.

WHY JOHNNY NEVER GOES TO TOWN

It was the boys who brought up the question.
"Dad, why doesn't Johnny ever go to town?"
Their mother and I look at each other
over coffee and wonder whether to frown
and how to answer the question we'd rather
no one would ask. "Why, he often goes with me,"
I say for want of a good answer.
"No he doesn't, Dad. He trims his own hair
with your ole lectric razor. He told me.
He gets his beef from our freezer and mother
buys his groceries. Not even to the fair.
He's been to the doctor once in two years."
"Now that's Johnny's business," their mother
says as she stops them from having their say.
"I want to know myself." I tell her. "Appears
he stopped going about three years ago."
"Then ask," she says with usual directness. "Okay,"
I say. But then, walking to the barn,
I weaken. I could go back tell her that I know.
He made me promise I'd never tell his yarn,
I could lie. But then I'd never know.
"Johnny, why don't you go to town?" I hear myself
ask. "Is it a debt or maybe some old sin?"
He looks up, puzzled, takes a horseshoe from the shelf,
pulls off his hat, wipes his brow, and says, "I been."

ANTICIPATION

AGELESS

Since the boys left, the tree by the game
room has come closer to the house,
pushing its green leaves, limb stubs at me,

scraping my spotted brown skin,
ruffling my thin grey hair
as I attempt to impose order

on the lawn it protects. Be brave,
I tell myself; I can trim;
I can run to one of those places

with room for three small pictures
on a scarred dresser. Nothing yellows quicker
than a photo album under a bed,

but the tree wants me gone to make way
for little brown feet, trailing to first base,
or using it as an out-of-bounds marker in the Fall.

You, darling, are out of time; I turn your pictures
to the mirrors where everything reverses. But
I can not find you. For other views, I go to movies,
the park. No one speaks. People hurry. Dogs
trot by, stick their tongues out for shallow, quick breaths.

Beck's Dead, Damn 2000

Not only God
knew the number
of hairs on Beck's head.
A few wispy, long, gray strands
folded on the too white pillow,
and golden memories flew back
like thick, black curls, convoluted
by rolled-down car-window wind,
strong as the hot-air ins and outs of his stories.

But with Melba Jean caressing,
untangling his twisted, curly locks
before school in his famous "Four-Stroke"
47 Chevy, I was ready to believe
anything he said about dark doings.
Impressionistic leather backseat covers
rose from indention's depressed witness
to hint what he would slowly confirm.
We lifted triumphs from him
like piston heads rising with explosions.

Beck buddy, when I slide in again
where you are, in the back seat,
I want some good tales.

In any heaven worth having,
Melba Jean is making you
purr like some big black furry
cat in her lap. For my prayers
and pounds of candles,
you fix me up
with the straight scoop, deal?
Swell.
Your stories make time speed by
like a souped-up Chevy heading for the house.

PROUD PROGRESS IN THE COUNTY

For Mike McKeever

Inbred, incestuous at worst, parochial at best.
we have become the fracking capital of the world.

Two sweet Pentecostal brothers, who mumble
in strange languages, carved tombstones years ago,
starving, started something new, a booming business.
They sold their souls for one billion and a quarter each.
Made some Chinese sorts waary happy. A little
"forward-thinking" town becomes a growth. The brothers
continue mumbling, now people strain to listen.

My neighbors cleaned, painted, bought benches, painted
primitive murals, opened "antique shops" to no avail.
As they are aging, growth has come groping dusty antiques.
The indigenous types smile, call it progress,
divine intervention, and believe.

Condos will appear draped in latter day "Dairy Queen"
decor. College graduates will swell the small board
of the Jr. College, think they are smart, and build.
More traffic lights will blink. No more a one-light town,
unfamiliar policemen will insist on parking either parallel
or head-in, not both side by side. The mayor will be one
of "them." Roads will often require closing for rest
and renovation.

We could live in Dallas if we wanted
"services," taxes, 24 hour traffic reports.
Too few tolerate bumpy roads.

Heroes go west Joe Campbell said. I'll follow
Shane's trail, join him if he will allow me. He will be
careful, think I am encroaching,
though he will understand me.

CLOSING TIME

When snow lifts off of roofs in silver swirls,
the wind dominates trees that bend
in supplication till roots show.
Birds swell, turn tail to the wind,
fight for balance.

Travelers hesitate just inside doors
grab at the remaining warmth
like women covering their knees
as if their lives depend on virtue.

The day does not hover even a moment
before the sky blackens. A pale passenger
slides by in a car, his face frosting the window,
as the wind gathers its own. Birds
pushed, try to rise above the sweepings
of white dust, lose their way.

Visitors, reluctant at day's end,
fly through a door they thought to slip open,
peep through, waiting for a better time.

DECEMBER

Today I bleakly look in a mirror
filled with Bosse's death,
reflect on George's emphysema,
Halton's forty percent heart, Bill's less.
Lawrence caught Lou Gehrig's
slow, drowning death. I see
myself alone too long. Laid out is the plan.

Come look in the deep my father calls.
I cannot run down to the dock
to sail in a rudderless skiff.
My sons stare at frosty breath
drifting over hoary caps.

Does the lighthouse beckon wind,
the tree call lightning?

FATHER'S PERFECT FUNERAL

My goodness, my father, would have enjoyed
his funeral. The driver on the road to salvation
in a stretched-out car lost his way.
Endless cars, some out of sight behind us,
turned into the same driveway to go back
in our search for the true church.
We met those who had followed,
waved vigorously, signaled
like a base coach sending messages
about the road to heaven. A serpentining row
of followers docilely turning-in, backing out
of the same pathway, continued a doubt-filled
journey. Mother shed laughter like memories.
The driver struggled. There was no stopping
for him. Those waiting at the church
looked down, afraid the earth might open,
pull them in. Those arriving smiled at the earth,
knowing it held nothing of consequence.

From the East at High Noon

For Jim, Lawrence

To those who are so far gone no one can find you,
know nothing this day is different from other days,
when the somber episode erupts a theme classical

as Joseph Campbell, vibrating the moment
Shane or *Hombre* recognizes his time
in the morning sun, says what all want

the sheriff to tell the Hadleyvillans. He readied
in his job, they failed, and nothing changes.
This message may float in space, never find you

who have seen yourselves reflected in the eyes
of Richard Boone, or Jack Palance, smiling over his beer,
but if it discovers you, know you are as clear as the credits,

out-takes, blinking to dark, looking like Gary Cooper,
throwing his badge in the dirt, ready to move on west
where all heroes have to go.

JUST LIKE THAT

Not long ago, twenty years maybe, only a few minutes,
a woman standing in a glass phone booth for all to see
was run over by a runaway boat on a downtown street
in Dallas. Also in Dallas, about a year or ten minutes later
a pedestrian on a street leading to the downtown area
was crushed by a falling car, an Oldsmobile.

After a tuna sandwich mother said, "Oh" as if she had flipped
a light switch and seen something she did not expect.
Without flickering, her heart shut down. At any moment
some little cell might turn traitor and begin
to gobble more than it needs for anyone's own good.

Only about three minutes ago, or two years or so,
a light plane struggling, crashed into a house
less than a hundred yards from mine.

My friend, Jim Linebarger, an Ivy leaguer and smart,
told me that my anxiety came from thinking one might die.
It is all so obvious. I know I am going to die.
What do you think about when eating a tuna sandwich?

MY TIME

You hold my hand that is yours
as I fall into the blue morphined haze of sleep;
I say to you dying people need to die
like sleepy people need to sleep.

Whirring machines may drown my words.
You never indicate you hear.
I may waste difficult words on you,
but I would fail anything for you.

Perhaps I'll lose you by moving on
to a realm in the thoughtless dark, but
I want you happy far from this antiseptic
air, looking for spirit somewhere.

If there is a mechanism for such things, God
knows I'll wait. Take your time coming home.

NAGGING

Poppa calls me into his room, glad to tell me
of mother's doings. She fusses at him
about his yellowing apple cores drawing gnats,
insists he eat his cereal, which she knows he hates.

He smiles, pleased, a figurative elbow in the ribs.
Mother thinks the woman all dressed
in white in the narthex flirts with him
because she comes to see him sometimes.

I know how she is, I respond. Yesterday,
mother was in the shower. Last week
she was in the kitchen. Today she is taking flowers
to the church. I'll talk with her this afternoon,

I tell him, set her straight. He nods knowingly,
man-to-man. On my way out, I take one
of Poppa's roses, drive the two miles out of town,
raise the bronze cup, place one flower for Momma.

OLDER NOW

Older now than Poppa came to be,
I see him, laughing, calling for me
to take that first step toward him
where he waits, looking straighter, stronger
than the day he first urged me to jump
from the high board at the club pool.

PROLEPTIC

He knew, he always knew, he'd die
during a moment in the pasture
when the herd's round, lowered eyes
gave neither notice nor inspection.
Grazing around him, steps sure
from finding life in vegetation,
their witless view of field's verdue
would stretch in blinkless selection.

He understood in his clapboard church
and often spoke in vacant old age,
of death straying to his ranch,
of angel visions, flimsy sages
of slaughtered time, to inspect
the bloody truth of God's Eucharist.

REMAINDER

Some measured day,
unrecognized
on a calendar,
I will meet death.

I greet every morning
with a firm hand,
nod politely.

Mornings rise
like rocks hidden in the earth yesterday
I throw at the sun.

As the evening descends,
I bleed fire, hurl epithets,
threaten darkness,
spit bourbon on the sea.

Time waves like vast spirits
lowering their sights
to ram me.

A maelstrom arrives
laughing out of the side of its swirling mouth.

Some sunless day my woman
will light candles
at the dark. My sons will look in the frozen space
of her eyes. They will see circles
upon circles.

TENDER MERCY

Almighty God
to whom all hearts are open
I know thee.

You desire for me to know
beams that hold,
fires that warm,
water that purifies,
has weight to crush,
power to burn,
ability to extinguish.
No secrets are hidden.

Cleanse my heart. I am
creation, not extension.
There could be no pleasure
without me. Your image
I am. I imperfectly love thee

THE LAST SUPPER

After the last supper
at the last resort
before your vacation
ends, pat your wife
on the knee, over tip
the waiter, hug
the cashier, kiss
the doorman, and laugh
all the way home.

TOO MUCH DEATH

(To take seriously)

Boys, sons mine, I want "Li'l Darling"
by the Diamonds PLAYED LOUD.
I want my middle finger raised
from the coffin, pointing up. Hire
an out of work actor to hit the Priest
in the face with a pie. Fill
the coffin with rocks and my main
remains. As for bearers of pall,
      find
a list on me of women
who will be surprised
to have been called on. Hope
they stumble, fall and curse
in mud to the final
swear word.   Pray
for rain, umbrella-ripping wind. Hire
a driver who loses his way
to the cemetery. Turn to him
to go back toward
the people in car line. Wave
vigorously. You may shed
a polite tear or two like sin
from laughter. Prepare
for surprises.
     Love

"What Isle of Bliss"

How unkind, unfair for everything, everyone
to rush into my past. I've slowed to a stop
to take it all in. Haven't I

bought a box camera, an Argus C-3, a Cannon—
stops up to 1/1000—and a Camcorder,
but they dissimulate. All, all flies past me as fast

as those I try to frame or put in a box.
My house is a weak memorial to books
and all I try to arrange, hold.

My wife has stopped with me as we watch
telephone poles sink, trees tumble, flowers fading,
zooming past as we sit quietly and look, tears

creating paths through dust. Noses pressed
to the windows never steam the glass. The air
is soundless as the baby grand in the living room

waiting for Christmas Eve. Our boys are gone,
all gone into manhood, forever. Nothing would do.
Sons fled like redbirds, hummingbirds

that will not let me ever so silently
open the plantation shutters before they flee
from bribes of seed, cool water.

I return to Yossarian, Clevinger, and others
close to their ilk who come round
to be as they have been. Scotch
sometimes slows things on this island.

WHEN I DIE

The field of stones polka-dotting the landscaped
cemetery should be surrounded with all the repentant, hymning
fallen angels who ever sent me more than a dozen rejection slips each.
In order to leave the gravefield of dreams, these legions must decipher
the meaning of my epitaph unanimously in secret vote.
Carved in a limburger cheese ball with a leather working set,
these words should appear:
He leaves life with you. Quick votes with electronic machines
elect the losers: the question is did he mean
he takes you with him to the next world,
or did he mean I'm through, you guys handle all this?
There is no right answer and all the wrong answerers
are hit with a penalizing jolt for daring to vote.
If they don't vote—two jolts.

Bury with me all the bad poems I ever wrote,
decided by another secret vote
requiring unanimity. Wrong votes are again punished.
(All votes are wrong.)

Bury with me the complete works of Shelley, Blake,
Coleridge, and *The Waste Land.* Include my thoughtless, harsh words
to bums, to homosexuals, and to the grocer who sold me
rotten fruit almost half the time. Next include a copy
of *Gone With the Wind* and my autographed picture
of George Reeves with red hair.

Have a chorus chant: *He's in the outhouse now*
to the tune of *He's in the Jailhouse Now.*
Throw a picture of two boxers in 1910 poses
with the heads of Charles I and Oliver Cromwell
imposed on them. Toss the picture on the dirt mound
and tell the rejectionists to image once again
the significance in their black and white minds
and vote on what I meant. Shock them one more time
and play *Little Darling* by The Diamonds at full decibel power.
Block the gates. Electrify the fence.

WHEN IT'S TIME

The only way to keep your health
is to eat what you don't want,
drink what you don't like, and
do what you'd rather not.
—Mark Twain, Puddin'head Wilson

When it's time to go
I want to know
so I can grab a breath
in an oak-floored pool hall
and wait for death
with a can of Skoal
and a case of Lone Star longneckers
while lucky old men play checkers.

WHERE TO SEE THE DEAD

Why do we see the dead
always looking down on us?
Or why do we say we do?
Haven't they another commencement
to make? Some new stage to cross,
some new world to be conquered in?
If not, they should close their eyes
wait until we do the same
then open to see us look them in the eyes.

Big Words, Pastries

Just before a final exam in Greek literature.
I hurriedly purchased a cream-filled pastry
From the *Amore* shop in the plaza.
Speeding to the exam, I slipped it into my coat pocket.
At my graffiti-profaned desk, with my coat across may lap
I caressed my pastry, surreptitiously extracting it for a nibble
when Helen joyously, gamine-like, plopped on my lap.

(A sensible man would have hung the coat
on the back of the chair, I know.
Strange what Athena, Aphrodite have us do.)

Helen without doubt felt something odd, looked on
my mess-filled lap, massaged her creamy butt,
misapprehended, hurled angry imprecations at the sky.
Such words are always punished, frequently ridiculed.

For the next two years, she kept her silence. Ten years
distant in a downward elevator in The Worthington,
we were together with our mates. Oh the fates! I spoke.
She did not. She turned away like Dido. You must admire
a world-class grudge. I have contacted Guinness.
            Hera taught her.

To her address in the Alumni bulletin, I have
mailed a box of gooey pastries every May since that elevator
meeting ten years past. I sign "Messmaker"
on a slightly altered reproduction of Thetis
with her hands on Zeus' knees, seemingly horrified.